WHAT IS THE ROLE OF TEENS
IN YOUR CHURCH?

Jawanza Kunjufu

Chicago, Illinois

ISBN #: 1-934155-49-7
ISBN #: 978-1-934155-49-3

Contents

Statement of Intention

The Role of Teens in Your Church addresses the needs of Christian youth, specifically those who attend Bible-based churches—not temples, halls, or secular facilities. This book was written solely for Christian institutions that use the Bible and that believe Jesus is the Son of God and that the only way to the Father is through the Son.

Introduction

The genesis of this book occurred during the summer of 2010 when I was asked to preach at a church on the following topic: "What Is the Role of Teens in Your Church?" I never imagined that in preparing for the sermon I would end up conducting such an exhaustive study. The Bibliography reflects only a few of the more than 35 books and hundreds of articles and studies I read. However, I can assure you that my sermon was shorter than this book.

Over my 35-year career, I have devoted my life to youth ministry, education, and youth empowerment. I have written numerous books for and about teenagers.

As a father of two adult sons and a grandfather of an eight-year-old, and having been involved in youth ministry for more than 20 years, my life's mission has been devoted to helping improve the lives of young people. I just love youth. I love the way they think. I love their energy, passion, and innocence. They feel there are no limits to their lives, that everything is possible, and I love that. They are exactly the way Jesus wants them to be, for with God nothing is impossible (Matthew 19:26).

I wrote this book because of what I call the "40-70-90 Teen Exodus": **40 percent** of eighth grade students leave the church. They are leaving *before or just as they become* teenagers. This alone should necessitate a state of emergency in the church. If 40 percent was not an eye-opener, read this next statistic: **70 percent** of female teens leave the church upon their high school graduation. Now if that did not alarm you, perhaps this will: **90 percent** of teenage males leave upon their high school graduation.[1]

How will the church function with just elders and young children? How will the church survive such a massive exodus of our best and brightest young people?

These statistics only reflect teenagers who are church members. They do not include the 34 percent who attend occasionally or the 30 percent who never attend.[2] In other words, these statistics are only looking at the 36 percent of teens who attend church. We are losing 40 percent of middle school students who attend church, 70 percent of female teens who attend church, and 90 percent of male teens who attend church. The other two-thirds of teenagers don't even attend.

What a crisis we are experiencing! Is America following Britain in church attendance? Only six percent of Brits now attend church. As a result, since 1969, more than 1,500 churches have closed in Britain.[3] Can you imagine, a country that was founded on Christian principles not only has lost its military and economic power, but church attendance is practically nonexistent. Is there a relationship between a nation losing its spiritual power and the loss of its economic and military power?

I'm concerned that America may be following in Britain's footsteps. Since 1962, prayer and the Bible have been taken out of schools, and look at what has happened since. School violence has increased, and academic performance has

Introduction

decreased. Our children must walk through metal detectors just to get to class.

When the attack occurred on September 11, 2001, people wondered, where's God? How could God allow this to happen? Where is He?

God is where you left Him. You took Him and His Word out of schools. You no longer attend His church. God never moved. You moved. You took Him out of your life.

If children and teens are our future and schools have lost their way, how will they be prepared to take over society? While many say the church is no longer relevant in our lives, I say the church is more relevant and needed than ever before. The church must once again become the place where young people receive the spiritual preparation to make a positive impact in the world.

I have preached at hundreds of churches where, especially on Youth Sunday or Family Sunday, the pastor mentions how proud he is of the youth because they represent the future of the church. Senior pastors and elders, do you see teens as your present or your future? How you truly feel about the teenagers in your church determines the attention youth ministry is given. If you feel that teens are the future, they probably receive a smaller portion of the budget and space and probably visit the sanctuary once a month or on special occasions. If you feel teens are your present, they probably receive the same amount as your adults and are in your sanctuary every Sunday participating at the same level as adults.

WHAT IS THE ROLE OF TEENS IN YOUR CHURCH?

One of the leading causes of the 40-70-90 Teen Exodus is that too many churches are living in the future when it comes to dealing with their teens. Too little attention is devoted to empowering them and they do not feel important. They feel the skating party or once-a-year participation in the main worship service are just afterthoughts. They are mere spectators in church versus genuinely participating members. As a result, they can't wait until worship service is over so that they can go home or hang out with their friends. Teens will not stay in your church long if they are only spectators. If teenagers do not see themselves in your present plan, they will not be available for your future.

Senior pastors and elders, is age segregation a fact of life in your church? Historically, racial segregation has existed in the church. Dr. King once famously said that the most segregated hour in America is 11:00 a.m. on Sunday. Can you imagine African Americans being denied entrance into churches? They had to worship Him in the balcony or basement while Whites were on the first floor. This provoked African Americans to create the African Methodist Episcopal Church and the African Methodist Episcopal Zion Church.

Gender segregation is also a problem in the church. Even in this present day, less than three percent of senior pastors are female[4]—despite the fact that the church is two-thirds female! There is also a dearth of female youth pastors. Preachers love to quote Paul's command in 1 Corinthians 14:34 (NKJV): "Let your women keep silent in the churches, for they are not permitted to speak; but *they are* to be submissive, as the law also says." Because of this one Scripture, some men have denied women access to the pulpit, the deacon board, and the trustee board. Is there gender segregation in your church?

Unfortunately, the same divisions and discriminatory practices that occur in the greater society also occur in churches across America. This is ironic, given that we're supposed to be the *one* body, not many bodies, of Christ. In this book, I will focus on the one discriminatory practice in the church that, if not resolved, will lead to the same decline in church membership that has occurred in Britain: age segregation.

Does age segregation exist in your church?

Are teens respected? Are they empowered? Do they feel important in your church? Have you ever asked the teens in your church how they feel about their church experience? The following are three simple questions you can ask them right away:

1. Do you feel important in this church?
2. Do you feel respected by the elders of this church?
3. Do you feel that your talents and skills are being fully developed and utilized in this church?

Youth ministry is church ministry. The two are interwoven. In visiting hundreds of churches in America over the years, I have observed that a tremendous distinction exists between youth ministry and senior ministry, youth church and senior church. There should be no division in the church.

I don't believe the problem is with youth pastors. Later in the book you'll read about the great work of youth pastors. I commend youth pastors and their ministries for the tremendous work they are doing. This book is not an indictment of them. When I mentioned the flight of young people from the church I was not criticizing the work that is being done by youth ministries. However that is not to say that youth pastors and youth ministries cannot be improved, and throughout this book we will look at ways to improve them. I pray youth pastors and leaders realize there always will be room for improvement.

Many of my findings and recommendations have been offered by some brilliant people in this field, including Wayne Rice, Mark DeVries, Alvin Reid, Jim Burns, and Kenda Creasy Dean. I have also lent my 20 years of experience in youth ministry and 35 years in education to the development of the Teen Empowerment Model you'll read about in Chapter 8. However, the last chapter of this book, New Wine, New Wineskins, is the most important. As Jesus says in Luke 5:37–38 (NKJV), "No one puts new wine into old wineskins; or else the new wine will burst the wineskins and be spilled, and the wineskins will be ruined. But new wine must be put into new wineskins, and both are preserved."

To resolve this problem we must begin at the top—with the senior pastor and the senior church. It's regrettable, but in too many churches the senior pastor, leaders, and elders represent the "old wineskins" Jesus was talking about. I'm not referring to age here but a status-quo type of thinking that excludes teenagers from being fully mainstreamed into all activities of the adult congregation. This failure is systemic, not personal. Unfortunately some senior pastors and church leaders are in denial. To them I say, if you have decided even before reading the information presented in the next few chapters that you are not going to change, I pray that you give this book to another church member who is more open and willing to change.

If senior pastors and church leaders refuse to deal with the 40-70-90 Teen Exodus, then this book will be ineffective and the problem will persist. If senior pastors refuse to take responsibility and, instead, blame the youth pastor, then the problem will persist.

A congregation cannot grow beyond its senior pastor. If the senior pastor does not believe in the power of prayer, there is a very good chance that members won't either. If the senior pastor does not believe in the power of words, that "death and life *are* in the power of the tongue" (Proverbs 18:21, NKJV), that you will have whatever you pray for (Matthew 17:20; Mark 11:24; John 16:23), that your words must line up with your praise, then the congregation will not believe in the power of words either. If the senior pastor does not tithe, there's a good chance the members will not tithe. If the senior pastor does not believe in speaking in his or her heavenly language (speaking in tongues, 1 Corinthians 14), there's a good chance the members won't either.

If the senior pastor does not believe in prosperity, there's a good chance the members won't either. Unfortunately, the prosperity Gospel has suffered a backlash in recent years, but throughout the Bible God promises us that we will prosper. Third John 1:2 (NKJV) says, "Beloved, I pray that you may prosper in all things and be in health, just as your soul prospers." The prosperity Gospel simply means that you are no longer selfish and pray that only *your* needs are met. Prosperity means that you and your family have all that you need and want and that you have more than enough to tithe and give to others. Not just teens, but we would all prosper in all things if only we were being taught the pure, undiluted Word of God.

The future of the church lies in the hands of senior pastors. Therefore, if we are going to address the alarming statistics, we need senior pastors to acknowledge that we have a problem, and that the problem lies in their office—not the office of the youth pastor.

I want to document my position at the very outset of this book. You will not have to go to the conclusion of this book to find out what I believe is the answer to this problem.

"A study was done documenting the long-term impact of dividing the church into age specific groups. The researchers discovered that people who grew up in church, attending worship and not Sunday school, were much more likely to be involved in church as adults than were those young people who had attended only Sunday school without attending worship. The results of this study clearly called into question our myopic focus on creating a successful youth ministry. If this conclusion is transferable to Christians, there is no such thing as successful youth ministry that isolate teenagers from the community of faith."[5]

If you don't read anything else in this book, then please understand this: the main reason why 40 percent of middle school students, 70 percent of female teens, and 90 percent of male teens leave the church is because they have been isolated in youth ministries and have not been made a part of the larger church.

In the next chapter, we will look at what the Bible says.

Chapter 1: What Does the Bible Say?

WWJD: What would Jesus do?

WDJD: What did Jesus do?

DWKTBWETKWWJD: Do we know the Bible well enough to know what would Jesus do?

The church marquees and bulletins of most churches declare, "We are a Bible believing church." Mark 16:15 says, "Go into all the world and preach the gospel." Some churches do not evangelize 10 blocks from the building. We can and we must do more to reach the 64 percent of teens who do not attend church.

It amazes me how churches say they are Bible believing, yet they do not have an evangelism or missions ministry. Mark 16:18 says, "They will lay hands on the sick, and they will recover." Many churches do not believe in laying hands on the sick.

There are churches that say they are Bible believing, but they don't believe in speaking in tongues. They don't believe homosexuality is a sin (Romans 1:26–27). They believe that people are born that way and that it is a lifestyle.

Some churches say they are Bible believing, but more than 90 percent of their members do not tithe. The Barna Research Group confirms only 9 percent of Christians are tithers. The average member give 3 percent.[6]

Do we know the Bible well enough to know what would Jesus do about teens in the church?

WHAT IS THE ROLE OF TEENS IN YOUR CHURCH?

What does the Bible say about teens? Nowhere in the Bible are the words "teen" and "adolescent" mentioned. However, we know there is a time in the life of a young person when childhood ends and adulthood begins. I propose we look to the Bible, in Luke 2:42, 46–47 (NKJV), for the age that marks the beginning of adulthood:

> "And when He was twelve years old, they went up to Jerusalem according to the custom of the feast. Now so it was *that* after three days they found Him in the temple, sitting in the midst of the teachers, both listening to them and asking them questions. And all who heard Him were astonished at His understanding and answers."

Throughout this book the age of 12 will mark the beginning of a young person's rite of passage into the adult congregation. This will be fully developed in the teen empowerment model. I believe the Bible is telling us that the age of 12 is the beginning of adulthood. Twelve-year-olds are able to think in the abstract. They are able to think logically. They know what commitment is all about, and they are beginning to understand the consequences of their decisions and actions. At 12 years of age, Jesus was no longer in youth church. He was in the temple with the adults, asking questions, understanding, and offering His own thought-provoking answers.

Chapter 1: What does the Bible say?

First Timothy 4:12 says, "Let no one despise your youth, but be an example to the believers in word, in conduct, in love, in spirit, in faith, in purity." Adults habitually look down on young people. They constantly remind young people that because they are older, they have more to offer. It is only in the church where the talents and gifts of teens are reserved for the future. In business, sports, entertainment, education, science, and all other fields of endeavor, teenagers are encouraged to develop and participate to their highest potential. Not so in the church. In Chapter 8 you'll read about some of the amazing accomplishments of teens past and present.

Proverbs 18:16 reminds us that our gifts will make room for us. Well, your gifts will make room for you (Justin Bieber, Selena Gomez, Venus and Serena Williams, Tiger Woods, George Washington, Alex and Brett Harris, and Dr. Keith Black) in other fields, but they will not make room for you in the church. Only in churches where teens are seen as the future are their gifts and talents not stirred up.

Paul admonishes Timothy, "Let no one despise your youth." Seventy percent of females and 90 percent of males may be leaving the church because they feel despised. They feel their youth is not being respected, that their gifts and talents are not being utilized.

> "And Saul said to David, 'You are not able to go against this Philistine to fight with him; for you *are* a youth, and he a man of war from his youth.'

> "But David said to Saul, 'Your servant used to keep his father's sheep, and when a lion or a bear came and took a lamb out of the flock, I went out after it and struck it, and delivered *the lamb* from its mouth; and when it arose against me, I caught *it* by its beard, and struck and killed it. Your servant has killed both lion and bear; and this uncircumcised Philistine will be like one of them, seeing he has defied the armies of the living God.'"
>
> (1 Samuel 17:33–36, NKJV)

As a youth, David was already a fighter. He already was experienced in defending himself and fighting for what was right. He was well tested for his youth. On the other hand, our teens have been restricted, segregated, and confined to youth church. I wonder how many talents and gifts we have lost to the 40-70-90 Teen Exodus. Remember, Saul did not fight Goliath. Saul's adult army did not fight Goliath. If anything, the adults were afraid. The only one who was willing to fight Goliath was David, a "mere" teenager.

Our neighborhoods are full of problems, and in the next chapter on trends, we will look at the problems of drug addiction, incarceration, suicide, teen pregnancy, and STDs. Goliath is running rampant in our communities. Instead of confining teens to youth church and pizza parties, perhaps we should unleash their gifts, talents, and strategies to defeat Goliath.

Chapter 1: What does the Bible say?

As Lamentations 3:27 (NKJV) says, "*It is* good for a man to bear the yoke in his youth." To bear the yoke means to willingly come under God's discipline and learn what He wants to teach. This involves several important factors: silent reflection on what God wants, repentance, humility, self-control in the face of adversity, confidence, patience, and depending on the Divine Teacher to bring about loving lessons in our lives.

This Word in Lamentations inspires and provokes me to realize that the best time to bear the yoke of the Lord is during the teen years. In 1 Corinthians 7:32–34, Paul says he'd rather that young people be single and without children. Why? Because the teen years are the best years to bear the yoke of the Lord. Young people are physically strong and able to think logically and in the abstract. They understand commitment and the consequences of their actions. This is a time when young people should not be burdened with secular and societal responsibilities. Let's trust God because they're ready!

Senior pastors and elders, if you wait until your teens reach their '20s to integrate them into the adult congregation, it will be too late. Remember the 40-70-90 Teen Exodus. The world is more than willing to stir up their gifts and talents if you aren't.

WWJD about the teen flight from church? I believe He would point to His own rite of passage into the adult temple at age 12 as the model for churches today. If you are a Bible believing church, then know that the Bible says your teens are ready. They are the perfect age to bear the yoke of the

Lord. The best time to fight Goliath is during the teen years. The best time to study in the main sanctuary begins at 12 years old. If we are truly a Bible-believing church, then we must let Luke 2:42, 46-47; 1 Timothy 4:12; 1 Samuel 17:33–36; and Lamentations 3:27 guide us into creating a new, empowering plan for our teens.

In the next chapter, we will look at trends.

Chapter 2: Trends

Spiritual
- 40 percent of youth leave the church by eighth grade.

- 70 percent of female teens leave the church after high school.

- 90 percent of male teens leave the church after high school.

- 62 percent of teens do not believe all accounts of the Bible.[7]

- Most teens believe religion is a nice thing, Jesus was a nice guy, and He wants them to be happy. They believe their obedience and sacrifice are not necessary.[8]

- 36 percent of teens attend church weekly. 34 percent attend occasionally, and 30 percent never attend.

- 90 percent of unchurched teens attend church because they were invited by a friend.[9]

- Two-thirds of teens believe you can be spiritual without going to church.[10]

- 38 percent of teens believe you can make it to heaven with good works and 22 percent believe Jesus sinned.[11]

- 65 percent of teens believe all religions are worthwhile.[12]

- 70 percent of teens say Christianity is out of touch with reality.[13]

- On most college campuses, Christian organizations have less than 10 percent of the student body.[14]

- In a study of Christian lifestyles, 84 percent reported that of the Christians they knew, only 15 percent had lifestyles that were different from non-Christians.[15]

- 20 percent of teens believe all religions have the same God.[16]

- 66 percent of youth ministries are populated by females.

- Many teens believe that truth is relative. They do not believe in absolute truth. They believe in being tolerant and open to all religions.[17]

- 33 percent believe in reincarnation and astrology, 31 percent believe in communicating with the dead and 21 percent interact with psychics and fortune-tellers.[18]

- *Only 6 percent of home schooled children reared in Christian homes leave the church.[19]*

Secular

- One-third of the world's population is under 19 years of age.

- One of four female teens has an STD.

- Most teens believe they can maintain their virginity while participating in oral sex.

- 10 percent of teens will become pregnant.

- 2,800 teens give birth daily.

- In 1950, only 30 percent of teens approved of premarital sex. Today more than 75 percent approve.

- Every day 11,318 teens will try alcohol, 6,488 marijuana, and 2,786 cocaine.

- 80 percent of adult smokers started as teens. 3,000 teens start smoking daily.

- 3,500 teens run away daily.

- 1,439 teens attempt suicide daily.

- Every two hours a teen is murdered.

- One-third of teens have been in a fight in the past year.

- More than 70 percent of teens report they have been bullied in the past year.

- Less than 60 percent of teens live with *both* biological parents.

- Teens spend less than seven percent of their waking non-school hours with adults.

- Many teens, especially males, watch more than 20 hours of television per week and play more than 15 hours of video-games.

- Teens spend more than $2,500 per year and influence more than half of all family purchases.[20] (All the above secular trends came from *The U.S. Statistical Abstract 2010.*)

- *This is the first generation of teens reared by MTV, BET, Facebook, Twitter, and text messaging.*

- *This is the first generation of teens that might never leave home.*

- *This is the first generation of teens that might not exceed their parents in academic achievement.*

- *While this book was under way, a professor at prestigious Northwestern University thought it was okay for a couple to demonstrate intercourse in class using a sex toy.*

Chapter 3: Framework

I opened this book with a problem: 40/70/90 percent of our teens leave the church. These statistics do not even include the 34 percent who occasionally attend or the 30 percent who never attend. Our first challenge is to keep the 36 percent who are attending from leaving the church.

After conducting onsite observations, interviews, research, and much prayer, I developed the following framework. The framework lays the foundation for the Teen Empowerment Model (Chapter 8) that churches can implement to reduce, if not eliminate, the exodus of teens. This Bible-based, research-based framework addresses the following core issues:

1.   Youth spiritual development
2.   The theological crisis in youth ministry
3.   Youth pastors and youth ministry
4.   The senior pastor and adult congregation
5.   Parents' role in the spiritual development of their children.

The framework consists of what I know to be true about youth based on my research and many years in youth ministry and education. This series of statements led me to an inescapable conclusion: in order to prevent and reverse the exodus of teens from the church, they must be fully integrated into the adult congregation, and their rite of passage must begin at age 12.

Youth Spiritual Development

- By age 16, if not sooner, teens will make a decision to either invest or disinvest in the church.

- Most teens in church can only tolerate being spectators for a brief period of time.

- Teens have an attention span of only 22 minutes for things they do not enjoy. Their attention span is endless if they enjoy what they are doing.

- The Bible does not use the terms "teen" or "adolescent." These are secular terms and developmental benchmarks. In contrast, the Bible has three life stages: infant-childhood to 11 years old, emerging adult 12 to 30 years old, and senior adult 30 years old to death.

- Teens are searching for a cause that gives them passion.

- This is the first generation of teens raised on Facebook, MySpace, and Twitter. This is the first generation that may never leave home.

- This is Generation I: Internet, iPod, iPad, iBook, iPhone, iChat, iMovie, and iTunes.

- Youth want a dialogue, not a monologue.

- Teens are not interested in sitting in the back of the pews, watching adults do everything.

- The best church volunteers are teens because as Paul wrote in 1 Corinthians 7:32–35, in most cases, they are not married and have no children.

- In the past, teens were expected to make significant contributions to society. Now they are expected to stay in school, avoid drugs and jail, and do a few chores.

- Adolescence literally means to grow up. Our society is delaying the process until the '20s and '30s. In the U.S., we call adult children *kidults*, England *kippers*, Germany *nesthockers*, France *mammones*, and Japan *freeters*.

- Teens have a new commandment for adults: Thou shall not bore us during Sunday service.

- Under the right theological teaching, church support, and adult mentorship, teens can become passionate about and excellent at evangelism.

- Teens need adults to listen to them, so when they are talking, don't interject with stories about your youth.

- In agrarian economies, teens become adults at 14. In our past manufacturing economy, teens became adults at 16. In a high tech economy, teens never become adults.

- Today's teens have seen 100,000 murders and 500,000 sexual scenes (90 percent outside of marriage).

- Since 1930, females have been starting menstruation six months earlier. Females are starting as early as 8 years of age.

- It is difficult for a teen to believe in a Heavenly Father if their earthly father left their family for a girlfriend who is close to their age.

- Adolescence has become a waiting period of enforced leisure with few responsibilities and little meaningful contact with adults.

- Adolescents who only know peers and not adults are destined to remain children for a long time.

Theological Crisis in Youth Ministry

- The crisis in theology is a failure of youth ministry.

- We must prepare teens theologically so that when they go to college, they will have a firm foundation and will never leave Jesus or the church.

- How can we expect teens to participate passionately in praise and worship when some do not know Who they are praising or worshipping? They cannot believe the Bible if they do not believe the Author.

- 70 percent of unchurched youth say the church stifles curiosity, makes people brain-dead, and is out of touch with reality.

- 60 percent of teens and 80 percent of college students have been taught evolution in school.[21] Most teens think churches teach stories and spiritual stuff and schools teach real stuff such as story and science. 62 percent do not believe all accounts of the Bible.

- Most teens do not know right from wrong because they do not believe in absolute Truth.

- Our society promotes open-mindedness and tolerance of different thoughts, beliefs, and lifestyles. This contradicts the Bible.

- 50 percent of college students who have been hurt by people are mad at God. Some teens are mad at God because their parent died and the pastor said, "The Lord gave, and the Lord hath taken away" or "All things work together for the good." The first Scripture ("The Lord gave,…") came from Job 1:21, KJV when Job was demoralized, not from God. God came to give you life and more abundantly. The second Scripture, Romans 8:26–28 (NIV), is not referring to negative things like your mother dying. It is saying that all forms of prayer work together for your good. Our theology must not only teach young people the Word, it must correct errors in understanding.

- Teens do not need more programs. They need a relationship with Jesus. They must learn the differences between religion and relationship.

- Teens who are saved, who walk by faith, and who acknowledge Holy Spirit as their best Teacher have a better likelihood of staying in the church.

- It is a sin for a teacher to bore children with the Gospel of Jesus. We must make the Word come alive. The Word becoming flesh and dwelling among us is the most exciting thing that has ever happened in the history of our world.

- God created sex. It's His idea. Satan has turned sex into premarital sex, STD's, AIDS, pornography, and abortions. No baby or STD has ever come from abstinence.

- Many unchurched people believe they can have a relationship with God (not Jesus, to be politically correct) without getting saved, going to church, giving tithes and offerings, volunteering, and following Christian doctrine, especially as it relates to their sexual desires.

Youth Pastors and Youth Ministry

- Teens know how to be teenagers. They want the church to show them how to be adults.

- Teens have video games, music, sports, and other forms of entertainment at home. They need the church to teach them about Jesus, not give them what they already have at home.

- The curriculum does not teach. People do.

- Jesus came to save the lost, not form a youth club.

- Youth ministry cannot be as exciting as a Hollywood movie with a $100 million budget.

- Youth pastors resign in less than four years. Youth volunteers leave in less than a year.[22]

- The best cure for boredom and the mass exodus of teens from the church is missions work—feeding the hungry, clothing the naked, visiting hospitals, tutoring, etc.

- Success in youth ministry should not be measured by today's attendance but attendance a decade from now.

- Youth ministry is too important to rest solely on the shoulders of the youth pastor.

- Youth ministries have mastered how to draw crowds for concerts and other events. The problem is they have not mastered producing disciples.

- We view youth ministry the same way a mechanic views a car: isolate and fix the problem. Suppose the problem with youth ministry is deeper than changing a program, staff, or meeting dates? Suppose youth ministry needs a complete over-haul?

- Ironically, the stronger the youth ministry the less chance youth will stay as adults. They have only known youth church. They have no affinity for the senior church.

- Some say the church is not equipped to heal children who have experienced divorce, abandonment, child abuse, sexual abuse, substance abuse, and poverty. That is only partially true. If the church can encourage youth to be washed by the Blood of Jesus, they can be made whole.

- Anointed music is one of the best ways to lead someone to Jesus.

- The number of youth ministries and their budgets has increased over the past 30 years. Ironically, over that same time period baptisms have declined.

- It takes 10,000 hours for youth pastors to become good and 10 years to become an expert.[23] Unfortunately, this office has a high turnover rate; youth pastors leave in 3.9 years.

- Youth ministry is not about entertaining or babysitting youth. It's about spiritual development.

- The solution to youth ministry will not be found in a leader, curriculum, or a gym. Preventing and reducing the 40-70-90 Teen Exodus will require systemic change.

- Do churches evaluate their youth ministries on quantity of members or quality of disciples?

- Is your youth ministry characterized by the following: unruly kids, unhappy parents, bad food, lock-ins, dilapidated vehicles, and burned out youth ministers and volunteers?

- Has youth ministry been reduced to rock bands, Halloween night, pajama night, pizza parties, roller skating parties, and shopping mall fellowship outings?

- Has youth ministry replaced the Bible and prayer with Xbox and Wii games?

- A fleshly appealing youth ministry designed to attract unbelievers can also corrupt Christians.

- We must develop a youth ministry that will meet the needs of our male teens, or the church will be 90 percent female in the future.

- How much of your youth ministry is involved with the unchurched?

- What is the difference between your youth ministry and the Boys and Girls Club?

- In a typical neighborhood, there are 3,000 youth, one high school, and five churches. Let's say that 500 of those youth are members of the churches. All five churches need to do outreach to the 2,500. There should be no jealousy or rivalry because there will always be youth who need to hear the Gospel.

- If the church were a sports team, the military, or a new business, teens would be in the starting lineup. Instead they are confined to youth church.

The Senior Pastor and Adult Congregation

- Youth ministry is church ministry.

- What is your vision and purpose for youth ministry in your church?

- Has a youth pastor been hired to run the second church?

- Are youth the present or the future of your church?

- How can a church build a $2 million youth building with a gym, plasma TV, video games, and pool tables but only allocate a meager salary to hire the youngest, least experienced youth pastor who will have few volunteers to help run the ministry?

- Does your church encourage teens to remain children?

- Teens have a lot to teach adults.

- Youth are baptized in front of the adult congregation and will not be seen by adults again until high school graduation.

- Research on the lifestyles of Christians and non-Christians found only minute differences. For example, 30 percent of Christians and 35 percent of non-Christians watch online pornography. 26 percent of Christians and 38 percent of non-Christians use profanity. 26 percent of Christians and 34 percent of non-Christians buy lottery tickets. [24]

- One-third of Christians are embarrassed to call themselves Christian.

- A senior pastor hired a youth pastor and gave him a nice budget. Then the senior pastor forgot all about that part of his church, the youth ministry.

- Are youth spectators in your church?

- Where is Holy Spirit in your ministry?

- Some churches have to hire security guards to keep youth in the sanctuary.

- Can you really have an effective ministry when the youth pastor leaves every 3.9 years?

- The most under-resourced volunteers work with youth.

- Youth ministry is everyone's job!

- Do gangs make your youth feel more important than your church does?

- Why is it so difficult to leave teen church and go to adult church? Does your church have a transition plan for teens?

- The church has tried many ideas to *attract* teens to church. Maybe we should use our energy to *keep* them by having them *be* the church.

- The greatest challenge to the church is tradition. Why do youth have to worship separately? Why do some churches resist women serving in the pulpit or on the deacon board? Why do some churches have men's week, women's week, and revival the same week every year?

- How much does your church value the "community kids?"

- Some churches think their youth problem will be solved with a dynamic youth pastor, committed parents, cute kids, a gym, big screen TVs, and video games. Sustainable youth ministry is not the result of a superstar youth pastor but the entire church's sincere commitment to youth.

- When youth lead worship, the congregation sees the covenant affirmed.

- Can we really expect college students to return to church if they seldom if ever worshipped with adults?

- Adult apprenticeships are far better for teens than peer pressure.

- Teen problems—suicide, drug addiction, and sexual promiscuity—are caused by adults (parents, educators, and church members) abandoning them.

- Churches don't want a youth pastor. They want the Messiah.

- If we are doing our job and reaching unchurched teens but ignoring their parents, we have won the battle but lost the war.

- Does age segregation exist in your church?

- Age segregation, like race, class, and gender segregation, illustrates a deeper issue in the church. People are more comfortable worshipping with people who look like them.

- Youth just need one adult who makes them feel special to succeed. Without a mentor, most youth will not succeed.

- Can the church survive with just elderly women, children, a few men, drop-off parents, and bored teens who can't wait to leave?

- The government will use teens to fight their wars, but the church will not use teens to fight Satan.

- Every adult is a teen with wrinkles.

- Teens who had relationships with older Christians apart from their parents were far less likely to abandon their faith.

- Some senior pastors try to make quick fixes with youth ministry, but have you considered that the very mission and goals of youth ministry need to be questioned?

- Do adults underestimate youth? Do we have low expectations of them?

- Adults are in the sanctuary and youth are in the basement. The adults have a budget while youth have a bake sale.

- Do teens have a greater leadership role in school than in your church?

- Most adults would not like worship if the entire service was geared to teens. The same applies to teens. We must design a multigenerational worship service.

- Most adults seem to be fine with teens in the worship service if they are performing with the band.

- Are your teens sitting in the back of the sanctuary? Are they actively engaged in the worship service?

- Would the situation be resolved if the teens sat with their parents? Is it a location or a heart issue?

- Jesus never said, "Take up your cross and follow me"—but only do so when you're an adult.

- Jesus never said, "And on this rock I will build two churches—one for youth and one for adults."

- Politicians say that children are their first priority, but because children do not vote, they are ignored. Educators say children are their first priority but they acquiesce to unions. Pastors say children are important, but because tithers at most churches are predominantly older women, the worship service accommodates older women first and teenage males last.

- Some churches are more concerned about Doritos bags and Pepsi cans on the church carpet than the spiritual growth of its teens.

- Is the church's greatest problem sexual promiscuity? Do potential youth members have a greater desire for premarital and extra-marital sex, pornography, and abortion than being members of a church?

- What percentage of your budget, space, and ministries is geared toward youth?

- Have we designed the worship service for the 65-year-old female or the 16-year-old male?

- Is your church doing a better job of imitating the culture or Jesus? Which has the greatest influence on the church: Scripture or culture?

- Five reasons for church stagnation are: tradition, personality, ideology, affiliation, and demonic power.

- Does age equal spiritual maturity?

- Has the church feminized Jesus? Would boys and men be more attracted to Him walking on water, calming a storm, and overturning the tables?

- When was the last time your Sunday worship changed? When was the last time the schedule followed Holy Spirit and not the bulletin?

- Do churches rely too much on a two-hour worship service to change beliefs and behaviors? What are members exposed to during the other 166 hours of the week?

- Church is not a place you go. It is a community of worshippers on a mission together.

- Even if churches are not able to do missions work overseas, they can still do missions work in the neighborhood.

- Attending church does not make you a Christian.

- It's not just teens who are bored with the worship service. Most churches are 60 percent or greater female. Many men are bored and no longer attend.

- Until June 25, 1962, public school students participated in prayer and the Bible was in schools. Since then we have replaced prayer and the Bible with security guards and metal detectors. And when there is a crisis we have the nerve to ask, where is God? The answer is where you left Him—outside of school, the bedroom, checkbook, and for many of us, outside of our lives except for the two hours when we are in church.

Parents' Role in the Spiritual Development of Their Children
- Parents can make their children go to church for 18 years, but unless they have a passion for Jesus and His church, they will leave when they no longer live at home.

- Most teens are sleep deprived, and they stay up late on Saturday night. Therefore, one of the worst things parents can do is insist on early morning service and expect teens to be energetic during praise and worship.

- Sunday school originally provided biblical training for the unchurched. Today it fills the gap for parents who no longer have devotion in the home.

- Some parents and church members think that the youth pastor's primary responsibility is to get youth to enjoy church.

- Youth ministry cannot be effective when it is isolated from parents.

- Most parents won't allow their youth to drop out of school because it's boring, but we allow them to drop out of church because it's boring.

- Drop-off parents expect the youth pastor to teach their children morals.

- The greatest gift a parent can give a child is encouragement to live passionately for Jesus.

- Parents, what is it about your faith commitment that has not taken root in your children? Christianity is contagious, but children won't catch it unless parents are infected.

- Youth stay at home longer but spend less time with parents. How can you become an adult when you do not spend time with them?

- The lack of commitment to God by youth is a direct result of a lack of commitment by their parents.

- Most Christian parents rely on the church to teach their children faith and Christian principles.

- Do parents want good kids or godly kids?

- Parents are in a spiritual battle with Satan over their teens. They will lose every time if they do not know they are in a battle or if they do not know how to spiritually fight.

- It's a challenge for parents and teens to worship together on Sunday when they do not worship, pray, or have Bible study at home the entire year.

- 92 percent of Christian homes do not have devotion at home all year.[25]

- Only 15 percent of fathers are spiritually mature.[26]

We will now move to the next chapter on the current state of the church.

Chapter 4: The Current State of the Church

The following charts paint a picture of the state of the church today.

ATTENDANCE	# OF CHURCHES	WEEKLY WORSHIPPERS	PERCENT
7–99	177,000	9 million	59%
100–499	105,000	25 million	35%
500–999	12,000	9 million	4%
1,000–1,999	6,000	8 million	2%
2,000–9,999	1,170	4 million	.4%
10,000–plus	40	.7 million	.01%

| TOTALS | Approx. 300,000 | Approx. 56 million | 100% |

WHAT IS THE ROLE OF TEENS IN YOUR CHURCH?

LARGEST DENOMINATIONS	
DENOMINATION	**# OF MEMBERS**
Catholic Church	69,135,254
Southern Baptist Convention	16,270,315
United Methodist Church	8,075,010
Church of God in Christ	5,499,875
National Baptist Convention, USA, Inc.	5,000,000
Evangelical Lutheran Church in America	4,850,776
National Baptist Convention of America	3,500,000
Presbyterian Church (USA)	3,098,842
Assemblies of God	2,830,861
African Methodist Episcopal Church	2,500,000
National Missionary Baptist Convention	2,500,000
Progressive National Baptist Convention, Inc.	2,500,000
Lutheran Church – Missouri Synod (LCMS)	2,440,864
Episcopal Church	2,247,819
Churches of Christ	1,639,495
Greek Orthodox Archdiocese of America	1,500,000
Pentecostal Assemblies of the World, Inc.	1,500,000
African Methodist Episcopal Zion Church	1,432,795
American Baptist Churches in	1,396,700
United Church of Christ	1,224,297
Baptist Bible Fellowship International	1,200,000
Christian Churches and Churches of Christ	1,071,615
Orthodox Church in America	1,064,000

27

Chapter 4: The Current State of the Church

There are more than 300,000 churches in America with 56 million weekly worshippers and many more members. The church is not monolithic. Some 177,000 churches have less than 100 members, which is more than 59 percent of all worshippers. More than 1,200 churches have 2,000 members.

We talk about the church, but what church are you talking about? Are you talking about a church with less than 100 members, a small building, and a worship service that includes infants, young children, teenagers, young adults, and elders? Or are you talking about the 40 churches that have more than 10,000 members, 20 acres of land, and a shuttle service that transports youth from one building to another? Some large churches have one building with more than 100,000 square feet, 10 floors, and 300 meeting rooms.

The church experience of teens will vary based on the size and commitment of the church. I want a church where teens are part of the larger worship service. The reality is that we have at least 177,000 churches that, because of their financial resources, only have one building. Some 135,000 churches have more than 100 members, and it's possible they have bigger budgets and larger facilities. Still, many lack a basement or a separate area for youth to meet. They don't necessarily want the teens in their worship service, but financial and physical limitations force them to worship together by default.

In contrast, I was invited to speak at a mega-church. The pastor took me on a tour. The church was so large that there was a separate room for each grade. It reminded me of a shopping mall or a high school. The preschoolers had their own room. The freshmen and sophomores were in one room, and the juniors and seniors were in another. My point is, there's a wide array of church experiences for youth in America.

Some of my peers in this field have advocated for an intergenerational church. In small churches everyone worships together, but that doesn't mean the service is designed for an intergenerational congregation. In reality, these are adult worship services that children and teens are forced to attend. I am not in favor of intergenerational churches that are really designed for adults. Some churches are implementing either an intergenerational church or they have one room for their babies, another room for young children, and the teens and adults are together. In Chapter 5: The Current State of Teen Ministry, we will discuss how in many cases the teens may be in sanctuary physically, but they are not there spiritually, emotionally, or intellectually. What they are hearing in the sanctuary and what they are thinking about are probably completely different.

Quantity or Quality?

Youth pastors nationwide are burdened by the need to constantly increase their numbers. They know that the senior pastor and church leaders are evaluating their effectiveness by the number of youth who answer the altar call, regularly attend, and give their lives to Christ. I sympathize with youth pastors. When your heart is focused on quality but keeping your job is based on quantity, it's very frustrating. I believe quality is far more important than quantity when evaluating the effectiveness of youth ministry.

The distinction I make between quantitative and qualitative evaluation in youth ministry is as follows:

1. Quantitative evaluation measures the number of youth members on the rolls, who attend regularly, and who participate in youth ministry events.

2. Qualitative evaluation looks at the *impact* of youth ministry on teens' lives. Are teens not only joining church, but are they getting saved? Are they being filled with Holy Spirit? Are they dedicating their lives to Christ? Are they maturing spiritually and behaviorally? Are they engaged in missions work? Do they evangelize? Do they bring friends to church?

I encourage senior pastors to begin evaluating their youth ministries with an emphasis on the qualitative. For example, let's look at a church that has 2,000 youth members but the youth pastor sees only 400 on a weekly basis. Of that 400, only 40, or 10 percent, are passionate about Jesus. Can this youth ministry claim to be successful when, with 2,000 youth on the roll, only 40 are passionate about Jesus and serving as His disciples?

Now let's look at a smaller church that has only 40 teens on the roll, but all 40 attend regularly—and 20 of them have become disciples and are passionate about Jesus. From a quantitative perspective, the larger church has 400 youth who regularly attend while the smaller church only has 40 youth. However, if we look at these churches through a qualitative lens, we begin to see that the size of the church does not necessarily determine the quality of spiritual experience. When it came to youth being fired up for Jesus, the smaller church had a success ratio of 50 percent. Under the leadership of Holy Spirit and the youth pastor, more than half of the youth became disciples. On the other hand, the larger church had a "success" ratio of only two percent (40 divided by 2000)! The smaller church is doing a better job of raising up teens in ministry than the larger church that has more resources, a bigger budget, and a larger facility.

Before giving a sermon, I will often find myself in the office of the senior pastor. That gives us an opportunity to talk. Knowing my reputation for youth advocacy, pastors will often brag about their teens and their youth ministry, especially when I'm there for youth Sunday. They love to say that their teens are the future and that the church needs them. They acknowledge that at some point the elders are going to die and that they need to make sure the church will be in good hands after they are gone. I'll nod and then ask, "What percent of your budget is allocated to youth ministry?" If the pastor is sincere about wanting to develop young people, he or she will give this question serious consideration. If not, the subject is quickly changed, and it's time for me to go preach.

One-third of the world's population is under 19 years of age. Let's assume that one-third of the church's membership is also under 19 years of age. I love numbers, so let's just play this out. You say that your youth are important to you, so it's fair to assume that one-third of the church's budget is allocated to youth—and that should be the minimum amount. If they really are important, then even more than one-third should be allocated. But the minimum should be one-third. You can't say that youth are important and less than 10 percent of the budget, square footage, and ministries are allocated to youth.

Has the design of your youth ministry been shaped by youth development or age segregation? Do you have a heart to raise up youth as disciples, or are you just separating them from the adult congregation to give parents a break?

In your building or campus, what percent of the square footage has been allocated to youth ministry? (This is a moot issue if, as in smaller churches, everyone worships together.) If youth are one-third of your membership, then one-third of your square footage should be allocated to youth.

What percent of your ministries are youth oriented? I love seeing churches, regardless of their size, that have Boy Scouts, Girl Scouts, Cub Scouts, Brownies, youth choirs, bands, junior ushers, and recreational activities. If youth are important and there are 30 ministries in your church, then at least 10 of those ministries should be for youth. Furthermore, they should be *active* ministries. I could write an entire book on churches that have ministries on the books, but when they meet and what they do are very suspect.

The most important question in this chapter is not contingent on whether or not your church has 50 members or 5,000, whether you have one building that is 3,000 or 300,000 square feet. The most important question is: What is the heart of the senior pastor for youth? Do you have a heart for youth? Do you have a heart for teenagers?

I am reminded of Jesus' love for children in Matthew 18:1–6 (NKJV):

> "At that time the disciples came to Jesus, saying, 'Who then is greatest in the kingdom of heaven?' Then Jesus called a little child to Him, set him in the midst of them, and said, 'Assuredly, I say to you, unless you are converted and become as little children, you will by no means enter the kingdom of heaven. Therefore whoever humbles himself as this little child is the greatest in the kingdom of heaven. Whoever receives one little child like this in My name receives Me. Whoever causes one of these little ones who believe in Me to sin, it would be better for him if a millstone were hung around his neck, and he were drowned in the depth of the sea.'"

Those words resonate with me, and I hope they resonate with the senior pastors reading this book. God is very concerned about His youth. He's even more concerned about senior pastors who abuse, take advantage of, and do not fully develop young people to reach their full potential. Senior pastors, God is going to hold you accountable for every teen in your church whose gifts were not stirred up and whose talents were never developed. The resources in His church, not yours, must be fully utilized to develop young people's gifts, talents, and passion for Christ.

Do you have a heart for teens? That is the essential question of this entire book.

Who is your worship service designed for: the 16-year-old male who may or may not give money or the 65-year-old female who is supposed to be silent but gives the most? Only you in your heart know the answer. This may explain why we lose 90 percent of our teenage males to the world.

Many senior pastors see youth ministry as a burden and one that must be delegated. If they have the financial resources and the space, or if they have members of the church willing to take on the responsibility as volunteers, they will gladly delegate their teen ministry to someone else. Once delegated, it is forgotten.

Kenda Dean, in the book *OMG: A Youth Ministry Handbook,* reports that "30 percent of congregations have a full-time youth minister. Conservative Protestants are 44 percent, mainline Protestants, 37 percent, Black Protestants, 41 percent, and Roman Catholics, 21 percent."[28]

I heard a horror story once about a senior pastor who hired a youth pastor and literally forgot that he had a youth ministry. He was that separate from it physically and emotionally. He delegated the responsibility so well that it was no longer a part of him. His church's youth ministry was not in his heart.

In *Best Practices for Youth Ministry*, Kurt Johnston provides the following excellent framework for analyzing the attitudes and practices of senior pastors, adult congregations, and youth ministries:

- Informed
- Interested
- Involved
- Intertwined.[29]

Let's look at each one more closely.

Informed. Are you simply informed about what is going on in youth ministry? Once a week or once a month, the youth ministry will usually report the number of youth that attended, how much money they gave, how many gave their lives to Christ, and what the weekly or monthly activity will be. At the very least, you know what's going on with your church's youth ministry.

Interested. Some churches, pastors, and members want to be more than just informed. They are sincerely interested in their youth ministry. If they see that in the month of February there were 100 in attendance on average each Sunday and in the following month it was less or more, they are concerned about that. If during the course of a month there was a decline in the number of teens who gave their lives to Christ, they are concerned about that. Because they are interested, they express their concern by sometimes visiting the youth ministry. Can you imagine a senior pastor occasionally delegating his Sunday sermon to another minister so that he can sit in on the youth worship service or even speak to his teens? This is an indication of sincere interest.

Chapter 4: The Current State of the Church

Involved. We see a higher level of involvement when the senior pastor and members of the adult congregation visit the youth ministry on a regular basis. Involved churches have a structure in place where the senior church is actively and regularly involved with the youth ministry. It may be that once a month youth and adults worship together. Maybe senior members chaperone weekly youth activities. But they are involved.

Intertwined. I am advocating for far more than being informed, interested, or involved. I'm advocating for the senior church and youth ministry to become intertwined so that there is no difference between the two. We will discuss how this looks in the teen empowerment chapter, but for now I'd like you to think about your church's level of involvement in youth ministry. Are the senior members informed, interested, involved, or intertwined?

I am reminded of one senior pastor who runs his church like a corporation. The members operate in the range of being informed and interested in youth ministry. Well, their giving was down, so a business decision was made to let the youth pastor go. The elders thought they could run the ministry with volunteers. It took them a short three months to discover that they could not run a youth ministry. They told the senior pastor that he needed to hire a youth pastor because there was simply too much work for them to do. I always laugh when I think about this story because trying to run a youth ministry can be a very humbling experience! This cautionary tale should give us more appreciation for all that youth pastors and volunteers do. It took the elders becoming involved and intertwined to realize how challenging, and rewarding, youth ministry can be.

Another church was concerned about the exodus of their youth, so they hired a consultant. The consultant conducted a survey of young adult members but only interviewed those who stayed. Remember, 40 percent of middle school students, 70 percent of female teens, and 90 percent of male teens are leaving. Why didn't he seek out the teens and young adults who left the church? It's as if we only hear what we want to hear! When we become serious and stop being in denial about youth ministry, we will begin asking the 40 percent, the 70 percent, and the 90 percent why they didn't stay. If I were that consultant, I would have asked the young people who left the following questions:

1. Did the church ever meet your needs as a teenager?
2. Did you feel respected by the adults in the church?
3. Did you grow spiritually at the church?
4. Would you have liked to have been a more active member of the church?
5. Did any adult ever ask you what your gifts and talents were?
6. Did any adult ever mentor you at the church?
7. Did your youth pastor resign while you were a member of the church?
8. Did your church ever teach you about salvation, being covered by the Blood of Jesus, and being filled with Holy Spirit in a way you could understand?

9. Did it appear that some youth were more "highly favored" among the adults than other teens? Did you ever feel left out of the "it" crowd?

10. Are you confused about your Christian faith *because* of church teachings?

11. Do you feel that the church made every effort to involve you at every level of operation?

12. Did you ever evangelize or engage in missions work?

13. Did church teachings make any impact on your behavior at school, at home, or with friends?

14. What would it take to make you return to the church?

15. What recommendations would you offer to the senior pastor and the youth pastor to improve youth ministry?

In my book *Adam! Where Are You? Why Most Men Don't Go to Church,* I outlined 21 reasons why men do not attend. When I preach and teach in churches I am always concerned to see mostly females in the youth choir, youth ministry, senior choir, and the larger congregation. I wrote my book about Adam, Sr., but we also have a problem with Adam, Jr. not being in the church. There's a 20 percent differential between the 70 percent of female teens who are leaving and the 90 percent of males. In other words, more males than females are leaving. There is surely no shortage of 16-year-old males, so how can we explain a teen choir that is two-thirds female?

In my book *Raising Boys*, I ask the question, do some mothers raise their daughters and love their sons? Do these mothers make their daughters come home early but not their sons? Do they make their daughters study but not their sons?

Do they make their daughters do chores but not their sons? Do they make their daughters go to church but not their sons?

I'm glad my mother told me when I was growing up, "If you're going to party all Saturday night, you will be praising my God all Sunday morning. If you're going to eat my greens, you're going to serve my God."

Has the church been designed for females and not males?

There's an assumption that Christianity is feminine. In fact the typical image of Jesus is effeminate. Wouldn't it be better for boys to see Jesus overturning the tables in His sanctuary? Wouldn't it be better for boys to see David fighting Goliath? Wouldn't it be better for them to see Jesus calming a storm? Wouldn't it be better for them to see Peter walking on water?

Can the church survive with just elderly women and young children?

Are we committed to attracting and keeping young men in the church?

Earlier I mentioned that one-third of our youth have been involved in a fight, and more than 70 percent of teens report they were bullied in the past year. What are we saying from the pulpit to empower teens, especially males? How does the Christian male teenager handle bullies?

Age Segregation

Before closing this chapter, I have one more question for senior pastors and church leaders: does age segregation exist in your church? Ephesians 6:12 (NKJV) says, "For we do not wrestle against flesh and blood, but against principalities, against powers, against the rulers of the darkness of this age, against spiritual *hosts* of wickedness in the heavenly *places.*" I believe that the same demon that is driving age segregation has also been driving racial segregation.

It is the same demon that is driving gender segregation. Not only do we segregate and discriminate against youth, but the same demon is driving segregation and discrimination against women. What percent of your congregation is female? What percent of your ministers are female? What percent of your deacons are women—oh, that's right. Women cannot be deacons in most churches. What percent of your trustees are women? What percent of your officers are women? Less than three percent of all senior pastors are female. Is your junior pastor male or female?

For some reason we don't do well with our differences. Whites and Blacks are different. It doesn't mean Whites are better. They're simply different. Men and women are different. It doesn't mean that men are better. Men and women are simply different. However, insecure people will rationalize bigotry and discrimination by saying, "Because I'm different than you, then you're deficient from me, and therefore I'm better than you."

The same applies to the age issue. Adults and teens are different. That does not mean adults are better. Adults are simply different. Senior pastors and church leaders, do you feel teens are deficient and that you're better than they are?

Jesus did not die for the senior church, and He is not coming back for the senior church. He died for the church. Until we become intertwined as a church, then in my humble opinion, Jesus is not coming back until we are one church with no race, gender, class, or age segregation.

In the next chapter we will look at the current state of teen ministries.

Chapter 5: The Current State of Teen Ministry

I've said in this book that the most important factor in youth ministry is the senior pastor. In this chapter on the state of teen ministry, we are going to look at youth ministry separately from the other two factors that have a tremendous impact on youth ministry—youth pastors and parents. In the next two chapters we will examine youth pastors and parents. In this chapter I just want to paint a picture. Just as the church is not monolithic, the same thing applies to youth ministry. Youth ministries come in 33 different flavors if not more. Let me describe just some of the youth ministries, without respect to size of budget, membership, or facilities, that I have seen and read about.

In one type of youth ministry, youth are in the main sanctuary, and they are fully involved in the entire worship service. In some churches, teens only serve as ushers, or they might sing in the choir as well. I have even seen youth give the sermon.

I've visited churches where the youth were in the sanctuary, but they had no involvement whatsoever. They sat in the back or in the balcony. Some churches have to actually hire security guards or ask the elders to monitor the campus because the youth leave the sanctuary and return at altar call.

Then there is the ultimate in separation: the youth church. The youth pastor and volunteers do all the speaking, and the youth are passive participants.

WHAT IS THE ROLE OF TEENS IN YOUR CHURCH?

Some youth churches have a heavy emphasis on music, such as Christian rock or gospel rap. After the youth have been ministered to by music, there's a brief sermon. Before or after service, the youth can hang out in the gym, play pool and video games, watch a big screen plasma television, and connect to Facebook, MySpace, and Twitter in the computer lab.

In some youth churches, the young people run the entire service, including prayer, music, and the sermon. The youth pastor and volunteers serve as facilitators in that they help keep the service moving.

One of the main strengths of active teen ministries is that in addition to Sunday service, there are many activities during the week and on Saturday, including counseling, tutoring, parties, missions work, concerts, and forums on sexuality, academics, leadership, motivation, home life, peer pressure, substance abuse—whatever needs to be discussed. Youth ministries do an excellent job of meeting the needs of young people throughout the week.

In his excellent book *Purpose-Driven Youth Ministry*, Doug Fields says youth ministries are trying to reach out to and work with five types of youth:

1. **Community.** Community students live within driving distance from the church.
2. **Crowd.** Crowd students are those who attend one of the mid-week or weekend forums.
3. **Congregation.** Congregation students have given their lives to Christ, but they are very immature in the faith.

4. **Committed.** Committed students not only have given their lives to Christ, but they are committed to developing spiritual habits such as personal Bible study, prayer, accountability with another believer, Scripture memorization, giving, and committing to the church body.

5. **Core.** Core students have discovered their gifts and talents, and they want to express them by ministering to others.[30]

I'd like for you to review the five categories in light of your youth ministry: community, crowd, congregation, committed, and core. Now look at the young people who attend. How many are community, crowd, congregation, committed, and core? What percent of your resources and attention do you allocate to each one?

I'm reminded of a youth ministry that was so impressed with this model that they tried to develop a program for all five. That is impossible. Another youth ministry wanted to reach out to community and crowd students, so they gave a concert. More than 1,000 people attended, and from a quantitative perspective, the concert was a success. Many community and crowd youth were in attendance, and the church members felt they achieved their objective. They had become attractive to the community and crowd. Unfortunately, they didn't think to include an altar call before the concert ended. So the report showed 1,000 people who attended on one line but on the second line, zero people who gave their lives to Christ.

We can't be all things to all people. With our limited human, financial, and physical resources, the senior pastor, who is the most important person when it comes to developing youth ministry, must decide how church resources will be allocated to reaching out to and developing community, crowd, congregation, committed, and core students. Remember my story about the smaller church having only 40 youth but 20 of them became core? Fifty percent became disciples. That is a very successful ministry.

Missions and Evangelism

Although the church has been mandated to go and preach the Gospel, missions and evangelism are missing in quite a few churches. Churches that do not have a missions or evangelism team are missing a tremendous opportunity to connect to community and crowd youth.

For example, let's look at a school district that has 3,000 teens who live and attend high school in the community. There are five churches in this community, and each church has only 100 teen members. You do the math. Now we know that some youth live in the neighborhood but go to church elsewhere, but to keep the math simple, we can say there are 2,500 unchurched teens who live in the community.

There should be no need for the five churches to argue over turf because as the Bible says, the harvest is large and the workers are few (Matthew 9:37). There are plenty of souls that we need to fish for: 2,500 to be exact. So there's no need for the five churches to fight over turf because Satan has 2,500 teens while we have only 500.

Public schools ministries are desperately needed. If your church feels led to do missions work in schools, keep the following ideas in mind:

- School is a great mission field that needs you as salt and light.
- Pray for the school and staff.
- Volunteer in the school.
- School ministry will take a commitment of time and energy, so your church should count the time you spend there as work hours.

Holy Spirit

What are we doing to attract some of the 2,500 teens? The concert was a great idea, but it wasn't followed up with an altar call. But let's say that on their own some teens became curious about the Gospel. How do we witness to those teens so that they become part of the congregation? In other words, how do we move a teen from community to crowd to congregation?

Remember, 62 percent of teens do not believe all the accounts of the Bible. Later we will discuss this theological crisis in youth ministry and the church at large. Often youth do not return because they cannot reconcile the Bible with the intellectual pursuits of college. If we are serious about helping teens reach committed and core, we must address this theological crisis.

Unfortunately, there are many ministries that are attempting to teach faith and the Bible without Holy Spirit. Note I did not say *the* Holy Spirit. I said Holy Spirit. John 14:26 says, "He will teach you all things, and bring to your remembrance all things that I said to you." Holy Spirit is a Person, not a thing. He's the Comforter.

I don't like the fact that prayer and the Bible were taken out of schools. However, if you know Him for yourself, then you can take Holy Spirit to class with you, especially when you have to take a quiz or a test. He will teach you all things. He will bring all things to your remembrance. You can talk to Him. That's why Jesus said, I did not leave you alone. I left you with the Comforter (John 14:18).

If senior pastors, youth pastors, and youth workers are trying to run youth ministries without the power of Holy Spirit, that could explain why 40/70/90 percent of our teens are leaving the church. If we want to develop committed and core teens who are sold out for Jesus, are on fire, not lukewarm for Jesus, it becomes crucial that not only are they grounded in the Word, but that they have a relationship with Father, with Son, and with Holy Spirit.

Why Teens Drop Out

In the excellent book *Already Gone: Why Your Kids Will Quit Church*, author Ken Ham mentions the following reasons why teens are leaving the church:

- Church is boring.
- Members are hypocritical.

Chapter 5: The Current State of Teen Ministry

- Church is irrelevant.
- They can get to heaven with good works.[31]

Let's review these reasons.

Church is boring. There's nothing boring about the Gospel of Jesus Christ. We do Jesus and the Gospel a disservice when we cannot find ways to make the Gospel exciting to young people. There is nothing boring about Jesus calming a storm. There is nothing boring about Jesus pulling Lazarus out of the grave. There is nothing boring about Jesus converting five loaves and two fish into a buffet for more than 30,000 people. We must do whatever we can to make the Gospel real and exciting to young people.

Members are hypocritical. I love that young people keep you honest. They want you to keep it real. They want you to walk the talk. They want you to be consistent. They have major problems with inconsistency. It's hard for a young male to believe in a Heavenly Father when his earthly father abandoned the family for a girlfriend close in age to his children. If we are serious about empowering teens, then we must be consistent. We have to hold each other accountable.

Church is irrelevant. Many teens say that church is something you do on Sunday but that it does not address the challenges facing them the other six days of the week. I also hear this in schools. Students learn how to add, subtract, multiply, and divide, but they don't understand how to use those operations in a word problem or real world applications. Unfortunately in some schools the skill is separated from the need. That's how in America you can have a BA, MA, MBA, and PhD and still be unemployed. You know how to work for someone else, but you've never been taught how to start your own business. We must do everything we possibly can to make church relevant and powerful in teens' lives. When we talk about Jesus, Peter, David, Esther, and Ruth, we must always end the discussion with how their stories apply to teens' lives.

Students think that history is boring because their ineffective teachers only want them to memorize names, dates, and events. But if you are an effective history teacher, you will always conclude the lesson with, "How can we apply this historical event to what's going on in your life or in the world today?"

They can get to heaven with good works. There's no work we can do that comes close to the sacrifice Jesus made for us on Calvary. The only way we will get to heaven is by doing what Romans 10:9, NKJV says to do: "If you confess with your mouth the Lord Jesus and believe in your heart that God has raised Him from the dead, you will be saved." I've heard young people say they dropped out of church because they got saved when they were younger so there was no reason to stay. They have fire insurance. They believe there's a Scripture that says, Once saved, always saved. But Jesus says, "'I never knew you; depart from Me'" (Matthew 7:23, NKJV). You can't honestly think that by giving your life to Christ when you were nine years old that you have enough fire insurance to keep you out of hell.

Chapter 5: The Current State of Teen Ministry

Jesus looks at the heart. You can't make a decision at nine and then ignore Him from then on. You don't consider Him when you're about to get married. You don't consider Him when you're paying your bills. You don't consider Him with your lifestyle choices. Is He in your heart? You're taking a tremendous risk if you think that because you got saved at a young age that you have fire insurance that will prevent you from going to hell.

How to Engage Teens

If we're serious about reducing and preventing the 40-70-90 Teen Exodus from the church we should carefully study the work of Doug Fields, author of *The Purpose-Driven Youth Ministry*. He provides a framework through which we can qualitatively evaluate the effectiveness of our youth ministries:

- Worship
- Ministry
- Evangelize
- Fellowship
- Disciple.[32]

Let's now review these.

Worship. How effective has worship service been? Is it anointed? Is the music anointed? Is the atmosphere anointed? Is it a welcoming, comfortable atmosphere for young people? Do young people want to worship? There are hundreds of books just on this one subject of worship.

David had much to say on the subject of music. In Psalm 150 he said, I will praise Him with all forms of instruments. Later in the teen empowerment chapter, we will discuss music and how the adults will have to compromise on the music selections. Young people want to hear some of their music in the worship experience.

David, the same David who killed Goliath and who said in Psalm 34:1, "I will bless the LORD at all times," was a warrior who unashamedly danced. There's nothing boring about warriors who also dance.

Ministry. Is the Word coming forth from the pulpit? Is it anointed? Is it biblically based? Are we rightfully dividing the Word of God? If our teenagers fully understood the Word, they would not believe that all religions serve the same God, that any religion can get you to heaven. There's no other religion that has a Savior who died for them, who is coming back for them, and who washed all of their sins away. Not only do young people need to know that, they need to believe that.

Evangelize. There are too many unchurched people who need to be reached. How much of your ministry is devoted to evangelizing?

Fellowship. Ninety percent of youth who attended church come, not because of a program, but because of a relationship. Someone invited them. What is the quality of fellowship in your teen ministry or the interaction of teens with each other? Remember, 70 percent of teens are being bullied. Can you imagine, we could reduce bullying with Holy Spirit-led fellowship.

Discipleship. If we are going to develop young people to be the core, committed, the chosen few disciples, then we must identify young people's gifts. We need to stir them up. We need to create an atmosphere that allows them to reach their full potential.

Is Your Youth Ministry *Too* Good?

Let me close with this very interesting statement: ***Ironically, the stronger your youth ministry, the less chance your youth will go to senior church.*** Let's review this statement.

In some churches the senior pastor has delegated so well to the youth pastor, youth workers, and teens that the youth ministry has become an island unto itself. Not only must senior pastors rethink their views on youth ministry, but youth pastors must give up some of the autonomy they enjoy.

Clearly the mission and goals of most youth ministries do not include transitioning teens into the adult congregation. Teens have had a great experience in the youth ministry. They have enjoyed worshipping and fellowshipping, within the nurturing atmosphere of youth ministry. But now it is time for them to become an adult. In fact, it is past time. Jesus transitioned to adult service when He was 12. This should be our model as well.

WHAT IS THE ROLE OF TEENS IN YOUR CHURCH?

Why is the 40-70-90 Teen Exodus occurring? The needs of many teens have not been met—or they may have been met too well. After such a wonderful experience in the youth church, they really don't have an affinity to the senior church. When they go off to college or the workplace, it becomes easy to put the church behind them because the church was part of their childhood, not a part of their adulthood. They never got to know those people in senior church. They were not made to feel important there. They only felt important in youth church. This is yet another reason why we must make plans to fully integrate teens into the adult worship service.

In the next chapter, we will look at youth pastors.

Chapter 6: Youth Pastors

Again, let me reiterate: most youth pastors are doing a tremendous job with limited resources within a program design that may not be the best for youth.

When senior pastors search for candidates to take over youth ministry, they look for the following qualifications:

- Strong leader
- Good communicator
- Excellent administrator
- Heart for God
- Love for parents and youth
- Degree in theology.

In reality, they often end up with a minister who is very young, the least trained and credentialed, and the least experienced. He is given the lowest salary, the smallest budget, the least square feet, and the smallest staff.

So I must ask the senior church, if youth are so important, why do you give their ministry the least to work with? Could it be that churches are looking for the Messiah to develop or miraculously save their youth ministries?

Over the years I have read many job postings in church bulletins and talked to many senior pastors about what they are looking for in a youth pastor. I am always amazed at the outcomes that are expected of the youth pastor.

- Create a viable youth ministry.
- Grow the youth ministry.
- Increase the numbers of youth members.
- Develop youth to be disciples.
- Help youth to enjoy the ministry.
- Satisfy parents.
- Raise money.
- Communicate well with the senior pastor, ministers, and church officers.
- Develop a biblically-based curriculum that will help youth have a strong foundation in the Lord.
- Coordinate all activities for pre-school, elementary, middle school, high school, and college students.
- Create a strong outreach ministry.

Think about it. The above list is impossible! It would take Jesus the Messiah to pull all that off. It would take the Father. It would take Holy Spirit. Yet we're expecting the youngest, least trained, and least experienced individual with the lowest salary, smallest budget, least square footage, and smallest staff to achieve those objectives.

Unfortunately, as a result of these unrealistic expectations, the average career of a youth pastor lasts only 3.9 years. It has been said that to become good at anything will take at least 10,000 hours. To become an expert in the field will take 10 years.

Unrealistic expectations and the relationship between senior church and junior church are two of the greatest challenges to effective youth ministry. It is going to be difficult to create stability if your youth pastor only stays 3.9 years.

Chapter 6: Youth Pastors

That means that a high school freshman who just joined the ministry might not see his original youth pastor on graduation day. A sixth grader who just joined will have a minimum of two youth pastors by the time that he or she graduates from high school. It's going to be very difficult to create a youth ministry, grow a youth ministry, increase the numbers, develop disciples, help youth to enjoy the ministry, satisfy parents, work well with the senior pastor, develop a biblically-based curriculum, develop activities for preschoolers, elementary, middle school, high school, and college students, and create an outreach ministry in 3.9 years. Each one of those objectives could take a minimum of 3.9 years just to develop!

If you think the office of the youth pastor (if he has one) has a revolving door, the average time a volunteer spends in the ministry is less than one year.[33] What is it about youth ministry that fails to retain youth pastors and volunteers? If senior pastors, ministers, and officers truly have a heart for youth, then they must address this critical issue.

Many youth pastors have told me that their greatest challenge is trying to satisfy and juggle the demands of youth, parents, the senior pastor, and elders. The top five reasons why youth pastors leave are:

1. Little support from the senior pastor, parents, and staff
2. Uncommitted volunteers
3. An inadequate budget
4. Youth ministry not valued as highly as other church ministries
5. Long hours and low pay.

If we are serious about strengthening youth ministries, then senior pastors and the church at large must address each of these problems.

Youth pastors remind me of public school teachers. Over the years I have spoken to thousands of public school teachers who have a passion for their students, but because schools are so poorly funded, they literally finance their classrooms out of their own paychecks. Youth pastors do the same thing. Remember, teachers and youth pastors are not paid like athletes and entertainers. But their love for youth is so strong and significant that they would rather do without personally to provide whatever is necessary.

Do we really want youth pastors to finance youth ministry out of their meager salaries?

If we're going to strengthen youth ministry and increase the length of time youth pastors are involved, then we must address the juggling act they perform, particularly with parents, volunteers, and the senior pastor.

Parents

There are two types of parents: drop-off parents and drop-in parents. Drop-off parents do just that: they drop their children off to church, and they expect the youth pastor to be *the* spiritual teacher for their children. Drop-off parents are also complainers. They're critical if the class does not begin on time, if the class goes over time, if the trip runs late, if the notice for the trip does not provide them with an adequate amount of time to prepare. Drop-off parents can always find something wrong with the ministry. The lack of support from drop-off parents is one of the reasons youth pastors leave.

Drop-in parents don't just drop off their children. They often stay for the service or activity. They encourage the youth pastor. They look for ways to help meet needs. They volunteer their time to call, email, and talk to missing parents. They willingly provide pencils, pens, crayons, paper—whatever supplies are necessary.

How can we encourage more parents to become drop-ins? Parents can either be your greatest liability or your greatest asset. It is going to be very difficult to develop a strong youth ministry without a strong foundation of parental support. I recommend the following strategies to increase the number of drop-in parents.

1. **Know the names of your children's parents.** Have you met your children's parents? Do you remember their names? You would be amazed at how many parents would be willing to volunteer if you talked to them and valued them.

2. **Call parents with good news.** Parents tell me they only hear from their children's schoolteacher when there is bad news. Like they say in the media, if it bleeds, it leads. I've been encouraging teachers to call parents with good news, and the relationship improves when there is positive communication. The same applies to the relationship between youth pastors and parents. I recommend that youth pastors and volunteers call parents with good news. Let them know how well their children are developing

in their walk with the Lord. Tell them how disciplined the child is and how nice. Parents have a tremendous responsibility, and all of us need encouragement from time to time. At least once a month or once a quarter, communicate some good news to parents about their children.

3.   **Have a parent appreciation dinner once a year to honor and encourage parents.** Hopefully drop-off parents will realize that if they want to receive an award they will need to get off the sidelines and get into the game.

4.   **Provide parent seminars.** Your children's parents may be lacking in spiritual development. It used to be that Sunday school was for the unchurched and that Christian parents were their children's primary teachers of the Bible and our faith. Unfortunately, many parents now believe the sole responsibility for their children's spiritual growth and development lies with the church, and specifically the youth pastor. The parent seminars can help them better understand just how important they are to their children's spiritual development. The seminars also can offer parents teaching skills so that they will know how to teach the Word, the Gospel, to their children. You can also use the parent seminars to recruit youth ministry volunteers. It's possible that some drop-off parents don't participate in youth ministry because no one asked them to. I'm in no way suggesting that youth pastors be responsible for delivering the parent seminars. This task can be delegated.

5. **Understand that even drop-off parents love their children.** You may like the children, but you can never love them like parents do. You can be critical of parents all you want, but you will never love their children as much as they do.

I try to encourage youth pastors not to focus on the negative and to think more about their drop-in parents. Even in the church we chronically think about the negative. If it bleeds, it leads. If there are 40 drop-off parents and 10 drop-in parents, who should we focus on? The 10 drop-in parents. They are the ones who are providing encouragement, resources, and supplies, and precious time. We need to focus on how the Lord blessed us with drop-in parents.

Remember, parents can be your greatest asset or your greatest liability. You must decide which one they will be.

Youth Workers

Research shows that the ideal ratio in ministry is 5:1— five youth to one adult. I could share horror stories about some youth ministries that have 50 youth and only one adult who just happens to be the youth pastor. Some of this, of course, is the failure of the senior church to provide adequate resources to the youth ministry. Also, youth pastors must learn how to delegate.

On the other hand, I've known youth pastors to get so frustrated that they simply give up asking for help. They are overwhelmed, disgruntled, and cynical because of the lack of support they receive, so they try and do everything themselves, which, of course, is impossible. Instead of training and delegating to the volunteers, who may not show up to help with an event or Sunday service, they throw up their hands.

Youth pastors leave because they are burned out. It is impossible for a youth pastor to work with 50 youth by himself and be effective—especially with the job description we discussed earlier.

How can the youth pastor's relationship with youth workers be improved? How can we generate more interest and increase the number and longevity of volunteers so that at minimum they will stay as long as the youth pastor? The ideal would be for youth pastors and volunteers to stay until they become experts, which would take approximately 10 years.

Listed below are strategies to improve the performance of youth volunteers.

1. Ask the graduates of your youth ministry who have returned as adults to volunteer.
2. Ask your current students to identify some adults they like, and approach them.
3. Ask parents for recommendations.
4. Always post a request for youth volunteers in the bulletin.
5. Ask the senior pastor to appeal at least once a month for youth volunteers.

Next, how do we keep youth ministry volunteers?

1. **Make them feel important.** I'm concerned about youth pastors talking down to volunteers, speaking to them disrespectfully. We need to encourage youth volunteers. As Ephesians 5:1 reminds us, we need to always walk in love.

2. **Assign youth volunteers a specific area of responsibility.**
Too many youth pastors see the ministry as their own.
They are very protective, and they feel they can do all
the work. To avoid burnout, master the art of delegation.
When coordinating events, there will always be multiple
tasks to get done in a timely and efficient manner. Assign
specific tasks to volunteers, and then manage their work.
Whether teaching the youth Bible class, hosting a youth
forum, or planning a retreat, there will be several areas
of coordination and responsibility. Let volunteers know
they need to equally share the load and that their work
is valued, important, and appreciated. You won't be able
to grow the ministry if you don't delegate or if you don't
let go and trust your volunteers to perform adequately.
Are you always covering for volunteers? Learn to
delegate and let go. Just understand that there will be
times when volunteers don't perform well, but that's a
part of the learning experience. When something falls
through and the children are let down, the volunteer will
clearly see how important his task was and how important
they are to the ministry.

3. **Set up the ministry to run efficiently in your absence.**
Youth pastors need vacations. Unfortunately, sometimes
they become ill. There are a myriad of reasons why you
might not be present at a Sunday service or event. If
you haven't mastered the art of delegation, things will

fall apart in your absence. Even something as simple as a meeting could fall apart. Every once in a while, let volunteers, parents, and youth run a meeting. Sit in the back or take a hiatus. This will be a great learning experience for everyone.

4. **Have a youth volunteer appreciation dinner.** We need to make youth volunteers feel important. One of the best ways to do that is to hold an appreciation dinner. It's even more effective if it's fully supported by the senior pastor and the church at large.

5. **Create an internship program for high school seniors and college students.** Instead of calling it a volunteer position, call it an internship. Work with high schools, junior colleges, and universities to establish the number of credit hours that can be earned. Invite students who love the Lord and who want to work with children and youth to participate in the program. An internship program gives the youth ministry a high level of credibility and importance within the church at large. It will also make students more accountable and responsible if they know their hours, participation, attitude, and quality of work are being monitored and reported to their high school, college, or university. Let students know that they can begin to build their resumé by serving the youth ministry well. Running a youth ministry is just as complex as running a major corporation or nonprofit organization. Getting practical experience in managing a volunteer

operation, building a membership base, coordinating events, running an office, raising money, writing articles for the bulletin, newsletter, or website, teaching, operating camera equipment, and assisting the sound engineer will make students more marketable in the workplace. With such a program in place, youth ministry will become an exciting place to develop gifts, serve others, and worship the Lord.

6. **Provide training for youth volunteers.** I could share horror stories about volunteers who were given tasks but didn't know how to implement them. They sometimes don't know the best way to communicate with youth. No materials are provided, no books, trainings, seminars, workshops, cassettes, videos—there's a dearth of information for youth volunteers. It's as if the only job requirements are to be able to stand and breathe. That is a critical mistake. I strongly recommend that the youth pastor or someone in the ministry provide training for youth volunteers. Allow volunteers to observe the operation for a month or so before giving them tasks to perform. If there are materials, have the volunteers read them. Be available to answer questions. At the end of the month, give a quiz to ensure that the volunteers understand what is expected of them. After all, they will be working with your most precious asset: your youth. They should be thoroughly prepared.

Senior Pastors

The relationship between the youth pastor and senior pastor is the most important. The failure to communicate, work together, and respect one another has led to many youth pastors either being fired or quitting in 3.9 years.

1. **There should be mutual respect and admiration between the youth pastor and senior pastor.** Again, I could share horror stories of youth pastors who left because they felt the senior pastor's ego was so large that he felt threatened by the success taking place in youth ministry. Some senior pastors feel that the youth pastors are trying to take over the church. Honest, open, and prayerful communication is the key to making this relationship work. Ideally, there should be a genuine friendship between the youth pastor and the senior pastor.

2. **The senior pastor and youth pastor should meet on a weekly basis.** Earlier we mentioned the paradigm: informed, involved, interested, and intertwined. Ideally in this meeting, the youth pastor and senior pastor are intertwined with one another. They should be of one accord when it comes to the mission of the church at large and the youth ministry.

3. **The senior pastor should visit the youth church at least once a month.** As we will discuss in the teen empowerment chapter, the primary objective of youth ministry should be to prepare and transition teens into the senior church. An annual rite-of-passage ceremony should be developed for 12-year olds. The senior pastor should work hand-in-hand with the youth pastor to

ensure that the 12-year olds experience a smooth and rewarding rite-of-passage into the adult congregation. From time to time, the senior pastor should also monitor the progress of the younger children as they approach the critical age of 12.

4. **Youth pastors and senior pastors need to sincerely and actively listen to each other.** Again, honest, open, and prayerful communication is the key to making this relationship work, and that includes listening to one another. It is possible to have a meeting and neither party was listening. They were thinking about what they were going to say next or about something else. There should be *qualitative* listening during all meetings.

5. **The junior pastor and senior pastor must work together to maintain the facility and transportation vehicles.** Youth pastors have told me that they've had great meetings, the numbers were good, lives were changed, youth gave their lives to Christ and became disciples, but the only thing they heard from the senior pastor was that there were Doritos all over the carpet, debris in the church van, and pop spilled on the floor. I'm not saying that youth pastors and volunteers should be oblivious and negligent about these issues, but let's be honest. Messes also occur in the senior church. The difference is that the senior church has a maintenance staff to clean up after the parishioners. The same needs to be provided for youth church. It shouldn't be the youth pastor's responsibility to pick up candy wrappers and potato chip bags after service.

6. **It needs to be clearly understood that the youth pastor has one boss, and that's the senior pastor.** Too many youth pastors say they were fired because the parents did not like them. Or the youth volunteers did not like them. Or the elders, deacons, ministerial staff, and trustees did not like them. This reminds me of school superintendents who have a nine-member board and have to appeal, comply, and acquiesce to all nine people. The same thing takes place in youth ministry. Youth pastors must placate many individuals and factions within the church. Keeping their job becomes a political exercise rather than providing excellent ministerial services to youth. If we want to develop a strong youth ministry and keep youth pastors, there can only be only one head, and that's the senior pastor. If the senior pastor is fair and governed by Holy Spirit, then we can extend the longevity of youth pastors' service in the church.

Before moving on to the next chapter, I want to encourage youth pastors. You're doing a fantastic job. I've noticed that in conferences, youth pastors ask other youth pastors to give them the secret to success. There has to be a silver bullet somewhere. There has to be a new curriculum, program, or way of doing youth ministry to reduce the 40-70-90 Teen Exodus from the church.

I don't believe you need another curriculum, program, or silver bullet. If you run the ministry with the anointing of Holy Spirit as your Teacher, you will want to stay—and so will your teens.

In the next chapter we will look at the role of parents.

Chapter 7: Parents

We could have an entire book just on parenting, and in fact, I've written several books on this subject. In this chapter we will look at parents' role in their children's spiritual growth and development.

There's no job more demanding than parenting. I don't know of any other job where you work 24 hours a day, seven days a week, and 52 weeks a year without a vacation. You are always being watched. You never can take time off from parenting.

It used to be said that the parental job ended in 18 years, but this could be the first generation of youth who never leave home. That alone should encourage you to take this chapter very seriously, because how well you do as a parent will determine whether your children will leave at 18 years, 21 years, 25 years, 40 years, or never.

The greatest gift you can give your children is not a Wii game, Nintendo, Xbox, iPad, iPod, a new computer, or whatever the next gadget will be. The greatest gift you can give your children is to model and encourage them to live passionately for Jesus.

In the typical Christian home Christmas is celebrated on December 25. Family and friends usually get together and have a Christmas party. Gifts are exchanged, but guess what? Jesus is not invited to the party. If Jesus came to your house tonight, would He know that you and your children love Him?

WHAT IS THE ROLE OF TEENS IN YOUR CHURCH?

Let me lay the foundation for this chapter. As I mentioned earlier, I love statistics. They paint a picture and tell a story. Listed below are some very interesting statistics and trends around parenting and the spiritual development of children.

- 54 percent of youth pastors believe the greatest challenge to their ministry is parental apathy.[34]
- 92 percent of Christian homes do not have devotion *all year.*
- 50 percent of children do not have their biological father in the home.[35]
- Only 15 percent of fathers are spiritually mature.
- 75 percent of parents allow their teens access to the Internet without supervision.[36]
- 74 percent of parents allow their children to dress inappropriately.[37]
- *Only 6 percent of homeschooled children in Christian homes leave the church.*

Furthermore, as the following chart indicates, influences on our children have changed over time.

1950	The Present
• Home	• Peer pressure
• School	• Music
• Church	• Television/videogames

[38]

Chapter 7: Parents

Let's now review each of these stats and try to learn from them.

54 percent of youth pastors believe the greatest challenge to their ministry is parental apathy.

92 percent of Christian homes do not have devotion *all year*.

Youth pastors are wrestling with the issue of parental apathy, the drop-out parent, and more than half say that this is the greatest challenge to their ministry. Earlier I mentioned that 34 percent of children attend church occasionally and 30 percent never attend. We're not talking about the 64 percent who never attend church. We're talking about Christian families that have confessed Jesus Christ as Lord of their lives. This lack of commitment goes straight to the heart of parental apathy.

Some people call these families "church Christians." They are Christians on Sunday for two hours, but because it doesn't take *all that*, then there is no need for the other 166 hours to be given to the Lord. I'm very concerned that 92 percent of *Christian* homes do not have devotion.

Notice also that these families do not have devotion *all year*. You would think that at least on December 25, before any gift is given, that we would acknowledge His birthday, who He is, and what He has done for us. Shouldn't we at least invite Him to the party? Before we exchange gifts, we should talk about our Father who gave His only begotten Son to us.

What a great Gift that was—the greatest Gift of all! You would think we could at least have devotion on December 25.

I'm aware that family life is very challenging. In the nuclear model, the father worked, the mother stayed home, and the children went to school. Today less than five percent of American homes reflect this model. Our homes are more like airports or train stations. People are running in and running out. There's the one- or two-hour commute between home and work. There's school, soccer practice, and all other kinds of activities, so it becomes a real juggling act. I understand how challenging it is to have dinner together as a family. It concerns me that family members run in and grab dinner off the stove. They go to their private rooms with their private televisions or computers. They eat dinner as they watch television, text, email, Twit, and Facebook throughout the evening.

I'm trying to make it easy. Let's start with devotion on December 25 before we open the gifts. Second during dinner, since everyone has to eat anyway, let's see if we can carve out a time to eat and worship together. Ideally we should find a convenient time to sit down and eat together every day. But if that's not possible because some people work days and some work nights and other logistical issues, surely we can find one day a week to have dinner together as a family.

When most of us think about devotion, we think that means listening to a sermon or reading the Bible. Sure we could, but we can do other things as well. We could pray together during dinner. Having dinner together is an excellent opportunity to have devotion. We all need to learn how to pray and give thanks. Devotion is giving thanks. It's prayer. It's reading the Word. It's being unashamed to call Him Lord.

Some families have family meetings. It's amazing that we can have a family meeting to discuss finances, the schedule, goals and plans, vacations, college, etc., but we don't have time for devotion. Either before, during, or after the family meeting, let's have devotion. We have time to do whatever we want to do, like sending text messages and emails. We need to schedule time to have devotion as a family.

I'm believing God that we can reverse the statistics drastically so that instead of only eight percent of Christian families having devotion all year, 92 percent pray and worship together throughout the year.

50 percent of children do not have their biological father in the home.

Only 15 percent of fathers are spiritually mature.

The first statistic varies among racial and ethnic groups, but on average 50 percent of American children do not have their biological father in the home. I've written several books about manhood, including *Adam! Where Are You? Why Men Do Not Go to Church.*

Now let's look at the 50 percent statistic along with the fact that only 15 percent of fathers are spiritually mature. What does this mean for our children? Not only are men not physically present for their children, but most who are present are not spiritually astute.

Spiritually immature men get going when the going gets tough. As our economy has changed, families have become more and more unstable. When men worked the farm or the line at the factory, they tended to stay with their families. Now that we are in the computer/information age and jobs have been sent overseas, there is less need for manual labor. This has wreaked havoc on the self-esteem of men.

But we can't just blame men's abandonment of their families on a bad economy and poverty. There are men who are gainfully employed, who earn six-figure salaries, and they leave their wives and children because of the lust of the flesh and the eye and pride of life. They leave wives of 10, 20, 30 years for a girlfriend who is the same age as their daughters. This is spiritual immaturity. I could write an entire book about fathers who do not make it to the finish line. How does this impact the spiritual development of children? It is difficult for children to believe in their Heavenly Father, whom they have not seen, when their biological father did not stay with them.

The greatest gift that parents can give their children is to model and encourage them to live passionately for Jesus. The second greatest gift that parents can give is to love each other, stay together, and model a solid, loving marriage. I'm not just recommending that parents stay together for the sake of the children. That's why Jesus said in Revelation 3:15–16, I'd rather you'd be hot or cold but not lukewarm. Jesus doesn't want you to be lukewarm toward Him. He said, "I stand at the door and knock" (Revelation 3:20). He's not going to just

Chapter 7: Parents

barge into your life and make you confess Him as Lord. Jesus will never deny your free will. The same thing applies to marriage. A marriage that's only staying together for convenience or the children is not much of a marriage. Children will see through the facade.

We have to be passionate for each other. We have to feed our marriages just as we have to feed our devotional time. We have to date each other. We dated each other when we first met. We tried to impress each other and put forth our best effort when we first met, and we have to do that throughout the entire marriage. Sometimes we think that once we marry someone, we've got him or her. It's like fire insurance. Once saved, always saved. I gave my life to Christ at eight years of age, and I can live like a heathen for the rest of my life. Some people think that once they walk down the aisle and say "I do" that they don't have to brush their teeth and comb their hair and continue to grow and develop and date each other.

I have written quite a few books on the issue of fatherlessness, and the research is clear and abundant. There is a correlation between fatherlessness and illiteracy, incarceration, drug addiction, suicide, grade retention, teen pregnancy—the list goes on and on. The common thread is fatherlessness. We could really help our children, especially our teens, have a much stronger relationship with the Lord if fathers were present and active in their lives. Ideally, every child should grow up under their parents' loving marriage. They should see their father loving their mother, loving God, and taking his rightful position as spiritual head of the household.

As I was writing *Adam! Where Are You?* I asked God a million times, "Why are you always on Adam's case? Did you not see that Eve ate the fruit first, not Adam?" God had to remind me in Genesis 2:16–17 that He did not give the instructions to Eve. He gave the instructions to Adam. Eve was deceived. Adam was disobedient. There's a big difference.

There has always been a war between God and Satan over the man. Research shows that when a child gets saved, four percent of the family will give their lives to Christ. When the mother gets saved, 17 percent will give their lives to Christ. But when a man gets saved, more than 93 percent of the household will give their lives to Christ.[39] Suffice to say, we understand why God and Satan are fighting over the man. **When you save a man, you save a family.**

75 percent of parents allow their teens access to the Internet without supervision.

74 percent of parents allow their children to dress inappropriately.

Unfortunately, there are many homes where parents did not encourage their children to live passionately for Jesus, but they did provide them, especially their teens, with a private apartment in the home. Youth today have their own room with a television, DVD player, Wii, Xbox, telephone, computer, iPad, and now they want a microwave. I'm beginning to understand why some children never leave. Why would you leave with a setup like that?

It is obvious why so many parents are not aware of what their children are watching on the Internet; the computer is hidden away in the child's private room. The average mother spends only 34 minutes a day with her children; the average father spends only 7 minutes a day. It's all too easy to understand how 75 percent of teens are able to visit harmful websites; they hardly spend any time at all with their parents. The same applies to their television watching. We could have a whole chapter on what parents allow their children to watch on television. They are not being supervised.

There are two types of parents: permissive and authoritative. From the above statistics, the majority of parents are permissive. They let their children dress and talk to them inappropriately. Permissive parents give their teens a private apartment in the home but only 34 minutes a day of attention.

Teenagers learn how to master their permissive parents. They will ask, "Can I wear these jeans? Can I wear this t-shirt? Can I wear this jacket?" They will ask 99 times, and they will be told no 99 times. They know that if they continue to ask, at some point they will get what they want.

Another example is getting children to do their chores. Permissive parents will ask their children to empty the garbage over and over and over again. On the other hand, an authoritative parent will tell the child one time to empty the garbage. He or she will tell them to mow the lawn, do the laundry, and wash the dishes *one time*. Authoritative parents have clear communication, and they are consistent with their communication. They don't change the answer, and the children know they won't change the answer. There's no need to ask them 100 times *ad infinitum* because they know the answer will never change.

Are you a permissive parent or an authoritative parent?

Permissive parents want to be liked by their children. Permissive parents sometimes wear the same clothes their children wear. They go to the same clubs their children go to. I've even heard horror stories about them sharing the same boyfriend.

Authoritative parents do not want to be friends with their children. They want to parent, not befriend, their children. Authoritative parenting establishes clear boundaries of behavior, which children really do appreciate. While a permissive parent may answer a question 100 times then cave in, an authoritative parent answers a question once, and the children know that's it.

Permissive parents don't have long-term goals for their children. Authoritative parents have a plan. They know where they want their children to be in fourth grade, eighth grade, 12th grade, even 25 years of age. They know where they want them to be academically, spiritually, socially. Authoritative parents are not only clear on the plan, they develop goals to achieve their plan and benchmarks to define when the plan has been realized. They monitor what their children wear and what they watch on television and the Internet.

Chapter 7: Parents

Fifty-four percent of youth pastors believe their greatest challenge is parental apathy. I suspect many teachers would say the same thing. Dropping off is an unfortunate mindset of too many parents. The youth pastor is expected to make the child a spiritual genius on Sunday, and the schoolteacher is expected to make the child an academic genius Monday through Friday. Even at home, the Internet, cell phone, television, and Xbox occupy children's time that would be much better spent with parents. Drop-off parents should realize that relinquishing responsibility to others doesn't help the child.

Parents, if you feel convicted in your heart about this issue, start today to change your behavior. Don't just drop your children off at church. Stay awhile. Talk to the youth pastor. Ask how you can help. Offer words of encouragement. Donate supplies. Try to get other parents to become more involved.

Influences on Youth

The influences on our children have changed over time. I believe the children of authoritative parents are less influenced by peer pressure, music, television, and video games than those children living in permissive homes.

Friends. Authoritative parents know their children's friends. They invite them over to get to know them better. They know the parents of their children's friends. They are cognizant of how significant peer pressure is. Amos 3:3 asks, how can two walk together unless they agree? Parents, if you really want to know your children, look at their friends. Sometimes parents are naive. They think their children are angels, but the fruit doesn't fall far from the tree. If you really want to know what your children value, what they desire, and why they behave the way they do, look at their selection of friends.

Music. Ironically, 66 percent of gangsta rap is purchased by White teens.[40] I wonder what percent of gangsta rap is bought by Christian teens. Authoritative parents listen to their children's music. As you're driving your children to school or even church, is your teen sitting in the back of the car with headphones on listening to gangsta rap? I've even seen young people walk into church with headphones on. I've always wondered what the lyrics were.

Television/video games. The average teen plays around 13 hours of video games per week, and males even more. Most teens are watching more than 20 hours of television a week. We can't find five, 10, 15, 20 minutes for devotion, but we can find 13 hours for video games and 20 hours for television. Parents, if you don't do anything else, you need to monitor your children's Internet usage, listen to their music, and watch what they watch on television.

I'm concerned about children who do not interact with their families. When they come home they go straight to their rooms to watch television, text message, send emails, and Facebook friends. Satan loves that. He loves to divide and conquer.

Chapter 7: Parents

At least one hour a day, have devotion and dinner together as a family. Instead of going to separate rooms to watch television, why not watch together as a family? Pick a show that everyone can enjoy, or pop a movie into the DVD player and watch that together. Have a family game night. Play Scrabble, chess, and Christian-oriented board games. One activity that seems to be quickly dying out is reading for pleasure. If parents are seen reading for pleasure, children will pick up a book and read. Reading should be mandatory in every Christian home.

If families spent evenings eating together, doing homework together, watching a movie together, playing a game together, and reading together, there would be no time to get into trouble on the Internet or watch inappropriate television shows.

Authoritative parents who are led by the Lord, who are trying to create a godly home for their children, tend to create homes that are reminiscent of the 1950s, when home was first, school (filled with prayer and the Bible) was second, and church was third in influence. Thank God that some Christian parents are successfully teaching their children to resist the negative influences of peer pressure, rap, and television.

Only 6 percent of homeschooled children in Christian homes leave the church.

This is such a fantastic statistic. Now juxtapose that with the fact that 40/70/90 percent of teens (who attend public schools?) leave the church. Just look at this contrast. Can we really put the entire blame for the 40-70-90 Teen Exodus on youth ministry or senior church when the solution has been in the home all along?

Only two percent of American children are homeschooled. Parents, if at all possible, you should consider homeschooling your children. If you want to ensure that your children will not leave the church when they turn 18, then homeschooling in a Christian home environment is the best solution. Why? Because homeschooling parents have complete control over their children's curriculum and learning experiences.

It used to be that Sunday school was designed for the unchurched. It was understood that Christian parents were their children's first and best teachers of the Gospel. Unfortunately, two things have taken place in our society. First, some parents have relinquished the spiritual development of their children to the church. Secondly, since 1962, prayer and the Bible were taken out of the schools and were replaced by security guards and metal detectors. Seventy percent of children are now being bullied in schools.

Parents who value education and spiritual development so much that they homeschool their children are 100 percent committed and involved. They are not apathetic.

I want to put out an APB to the 94 percent. What was it about the Christian homeschooling experience that motivated you to stay in church? Will you raise your children the same way? I almost could end the book here because homeschooling is such a powerful way to remedy the 40-70-90 Teen Exodus from church. We need more parents to homeschool their children in a Christian home environment.

Let's review the homeschooling numbers.

- Of the 100 million children in America, approximately 2 million children are homeschooled, or 2 percent.
- If 36 percent of American families attend church, then that means there are potentially 36 million children who attend church.

As you can see, the harvest is large. Thirty-four million (36 minus 2 who are homeschooled) children being reared as Christians are sent to schools where Jesus is not revered as Lord and prayer and the Bible have been removed. We won't even begin to talk about the other 64 million children who are *not* being reared in Christian homes and who attend schools without the Bible and prayer.

I am aware that most Christian parents feel that homeschooling is not an option. Until more parents join the ranks of homeschooling families, or at minimum, they reclaim their role as first and best teachers of the Gospel, they will continue to depend on youth ministry for their children's spiritual growth and development.

Parents, do you want good kids or godly kids? Proverbs 18:21 tells us that "Death and life *are* in the power of the tongue." In Mark 11:24 Jesus says that we will have whatever we pray for. If you don't *say* you want godly kids, then you won't have them. If you simply want kids who stay out of jail, do reasonably well in school, only tell little white lies, get a job and marry and have children and buy a house and believe they can get to heaven because they give to charity and they help their neighbor, then that's what you will have.

Satan hates families. He hates fathers, he hates mothers, and he really hates your children. He will do everything he possibly can to separate mothers from fathers, have parents be permissive, and raise your children on the Internet, television, and video games. If you want godly children, you have to know that you are in a war. You can't win a war if you don't know you're in one. It is even more difficult to win a war when you don't know the enemy. Ephesians 6:11-19 talks about the war.

It is impossible to win a war when you don't know what your weapons are. According to Ephesians 6, we're in a spiritual war. "For we do not wrestle against flesh and blood, but against principalities, against powers, against the rulers of the darkness of this age, against spiritual *hosts* of wickedness in the heavenly *places*" (Ephesians 6:12, NKJV).

Parents, if you're going to protect your children against Satan, there are several things you're going to have to do.

1. **Put on the full armor of God** (as described in Ephesians 6).
2. **Know the Bible and use it as a sword.** When Satan tried to tempt Jesus, Jesus kept saying, "It is written." You need to know what is written so that every time Satan throws a dart at you or your children, you'll know what is written to address that.

Chapter 7: Parents

3. **Know that you have authority.** In Matthew 18:18, "Whatever you bind on earth will be bound in heaven, and whatever you loose on earth will be loosed in heaven." God has given you authority. You have to bind, and you have to loose.

4. **Pray with authority.** You need to know not only the power of prayer but the power of intercessory prayer. The one will send a thousand to flight, and two will send 10,000 to flight (Deuteronomy 32:30). That's why it's so important to have devotion together as a family; your power increases exponentially.

5. **Know that death and life are in the power of the tongue.** You do not get what you pray for. You get what you *say*. People will pray and believe they are healed, and they thank God at the altar that they are healed of their illness. Then when they leave church and go home, they get on the phone and tell their friends all about their illness. Which one is it? In church you said you were healed. On the telephone with your friends you acknowledged the illness. It's important to keep your words consistent with your prayers.

6. **Plead the Blood of Jesus over you and your family.** There is power in the Blood.

7. **Read and understand John 14:15–18.** Jesus said, I did not leave you alone, but I left you with a Comforter who will teach you all things and bring all things to your remembrance.

WHAT IS THE ROLE OF TEENS IN YOUR CHURCH?

We could have an entire book just on Satan hating you, your family, and your children and what you must to do fight for your children. For now I'll just say, read your Bible.

The second most important chapter in this book is next; we will examine the teen empowerment model. The most important chapter is Chapter 9: New Wine, New Wineskins.

Chapter 8: Teen Empowerment Model

Throughout this book we have learned about some of the many reasons behind the 40-70-90 Teen Exodus, and now in this chapter I will propose a model that churches and youth ministries can use to reduce this flight. Churches should consider forming a strategic planning committee to discuss these issues and develop plans for change. I humbly have offered the vision for this change: *integration of teens into the main sanctuary so that they can worship together with adults*. Your planning team will develop the goals, objectives, activities, timelines, and budget for designing and implementing the changes.

You will find that some of the ideas in this chapter will challenge the existing mindset of some team members. This may cause stress, but if we are to stem the tide of youth from the church, we must realize that neglecting our teens, and keeping them in a childlike stage of development will not sustain the growth of the church. We must begin to change our thinking around this issue.

The planning committee should include the following individuals: senior pastor, youth pastor, church leaders, parents, parishioners, young adults (current and former members), and especially teens. When working with schools, I am always amazed when educators engage in planning activities for youth without including youth on their committees! Not only will including teens in discussions and planning activities provide valuable input on how youth ministry can be improved, teens will begin to feel appreciated for their contribution.

The Bible-based, research-based Teen Empowerment Model is based on the framework I presented in Chapter 3 and contains two main planning areas:

1.   Preparing and transitioning youth for adult worship.
2.   The new role of the youth pastor and youth ministry.

This model proposes many changes to the way churches think and function, so don't try and take on everything at once. I recommend choosing one or two activities in each of the planning areas to work on.

The planning team should be led by Holy Spirit and the vision of the senior pastor. Meetings should always begin with prayer and be conducted in love and respect for one another.

Most importantly, the implementation of this Teen Empowerment Model assumes that your church agrees with integrating 12-year-olds and teens into the adult congregation. This model is *not* about developing nice youth ministry activities for teens. There are already plenty of those. The Teen Empowerment Model is about helping them grow into mature adults as Jesus began to do at age 12. For many churches, this will require a lot of soul searching regarding the way they look at teens and youth ministry.

And finally, the planning team should communicate with the adult congregation about the major changes that will take place. This should be done in a spirit of joy and celebration!

Chapter 8: Teen Empowerment Model

Preparing and Transitioning Youth for Adult Worship

One of the most important studies that was ever conducted on teens and the church discovered that dividing the church into age-specific groups has an unintended long-term impact.

> "The researchers discovered that people who grew up in church attending worship and not Sunday school were much more likely to be involved in church as adults than were those young people who attended only Sunday school without attending worship. The results of this study clearly call into question our myopic focus on creating a successful youth ministry." (Mark DeVries, *Family-Based Youth Ministry,* p. 102)

I agree with the findings, but I disagree with the researchers' conclusion—getting rid of youth ministry. If we think about youth ministry as the department of the church that focuses on training youth for their inevitable entrance into the adult congregation, then clearly we can begin to see how important it is to the church as a whole.

Children. Nowhere in the Bible are the terms "teenagers" or "adolescents" mentioned. The Bible divides people into three age groups:

- Children – infants to 11
- Young adults – 12 to 30
- Elders – 30 through death.

Some of my peers have recommended that not only do we need to abolish youth ministry, we need to abolish children's ministry and have everyone worship together. I disagree. There are some aspects of adult worship that are too advanced for children. They become bored, restless, and frustrated when they are forced to sit still and listen. Many just go to sleep. Under the Teen Empowerment Model, the goal of children's worship would be to prepare children, using an age-appropriate curriculum, for their rite-of-passage into the adult congregation at the age of 12.

Children (infants to 11) should worship in a separate area because, in general, they have short attention spans, cannot think in the abstract, and do not fully understand the consequences of their decisions or the seriousness of commitment. Of course, this does not mean that there are no exceptions to the rule. There are numerous examples of young children who can think in the abstract, understand the consequences of their decisions, make a commitment, and have long attention spans. On the other side of the coin, we have 40-year-olds with short attention spans who do not understand the consequences of their decisions—especially men who leave their wives after many years for girlfriends half their age.

Now there are many ways churches can go about preparing and training children. Some churches bring their young children into the sanctuary for praise and worship and then release them for their own sermon. I can appreciate and accept that approach, just as long as they can go to a separate area

Chapter 8: Teen Empowerment Model

for their own age-appropriate sermon. I don't agree with the intergenerational approach for sermons, Sunday school, and Bible study.

Some small churches have intergenerational services, but they have them by default. Members have no choice but to worship together because there are no other facilities where the children and teens could go. Just because children and teens are in the main sanctuary for the entire service does not mean that their spiritual needs are being met. Usually they are not. I would strongly encourage such churches to look for ways to make the services appropriate for children, teens, *and* adults. Otherwise, the children will just go to sleep or fidget. Your teens will sit in the back, sneak outside if they can, and long for the day when they don't have to come back.

Teens. I am a big fan of rites-of-passage programs, and I would encourage your church to develop one to mark the graduation of your 12-year-olds and teens from youth ministry and their entrance into the adult congregation. This annual event can take place in the main sanctuary after Sunday service. The ceremony can include giving the graduates certificates and/or gifts (e.g., a Bible). The senior pastor and youth pastor should speak and present the certificates together. A program can be printed that lists the graduates and the adult ministries they will serve. In honor of the graduates, there should be music and an air of joyful celebration.

Once the graduates are integrated into the main church, adult mentors should work with them to ensure that they understand what is going on. The idea of teens worshipping with adults is not new. Jim Burns (*Uncommon Youth Ministry*), Alvin Reid (*Raising the Bar*), Wayne Rice (*Reinventing Youth Ministry (Again)*), Mark DeVries (*Family-Based Youth Ministry*), and Drew Dyck (*Generation Ex-Christian*) all recommend that teens should worship with adults. And as Dyck states, "Those young people who had relationships with older Christians were far less likely to abandon their faith."[41]

With so many recommending this "best practice," I wonder why it hasn't been implemented in more churches. When will we become both hearers and doers of the Word? How long will we refuse to accept that we have a crisis on our hands?

Some churches have a teen-adult church on the fifth Sunday of the month. Notice the fifth Sunday. My point is that we say that youth are important, but in practice, they are not a priority.

Some churches are a little different. They have teens "visit" the first, second, third, or fourth Sunday of the month. I've preached in many services like this. What really concerns me is that some adult members do not attend church on youth Sunday. They go visit another church, or they don't attend church at all. How ludicrous, but unfortunately this takes place more often than you can imagine.

I've been to other churches where youth give the sermon on Youth Sunday. As much as I'm advocating youth empowerment, I don't agree with teenagers giving the sermon. Let me offer a scenario.

The senior pastor of this particular church is well-trained in theology. He has devoted his life to the Gospel and the preparation of sermons. Fifth Sunday has been designated Youth Sunday. How many fifth Sundays are in a year? Not many. On that day, the senior pastor is asked to step down so that a teenager, who has less than one month to prepare, can stand at the pulpit and deliver a powerful Word. I don't think that's a wise decision, and it does not serve the congregation very well either.

Let's go further. I know senior pastors who have quite a few ministers on staff, and they are all well trained. All are graduates of Bible college or seminary. Please don't misquote me and think that I believe the only qualification to give the sermon is that you must be a graduate of a Bible college or seminary school. There are too many examples of pastors who are graduates of Bible colleges or seminaries, but they are not rightly dividing the Word (2 Timothy 2:15), there is no anointing, and Holy Spirit is not present and the congregation is not being fed properly. That's another book. My point is that members of the ministerial staff seldom have the opportunity to give the sermon, and we are going to skip over them to give the pulpit over to an untrained teenager? I appreciate the desire to empower youth, but I believe the Word should be delivered by an experienced minister with a calling on his or her life.

My model offers numerous other ways to empower youth. I am recommending that teenagers are involved in *all other aspects* of the worship service, including the following:

- Parking lot attendant
- Security guard

- Greeter
- Usher
- Praise and worship team
- Selection of music
- All choirs
- Band
- Give announcements
- Read the Scriptures
- Give the prayer
- Trustee
- Armor bearer
- Dance and drama ministry
- Media department
- Deacon.

I thought long and hard about whether to include "deacon" on the list. But because I may never see you again, because you may never read another of my books, I wanted to challenge you on what could be the last bastion of elder power in the church. If a church does not allow women to serve as deacons and senior or youth pastors, they surely will not let teenagers serve as deacons. These elders are quick to remind us of 1Timothy 3:1–13, the Scripture that describes the qualifications of deacons.

For example, the deacon is to be the husband of one wife. This Scripture is used to rationalize that only a married *man* can serve in this office. Are you sure you want to be that literal in the translation of the Word and not allow Holy Spirit to be our Teacher? Let's dissect this. The deacon is to be the husband of one wife. This means that you cannot be a deacon unless you're married. For all those reading this book, I want you to review your deacon list. Any male deacon who is not married needs to be removed.

Are there any divorced deacons in your church? Taken literally, "one wife" means that the deacon cannot have been divorced. That's more than one wife. Any male deacon in your church who has been divorced must be removed.

The Scripture states that the deacon must handle himself properly in family activities, which means that any deacon who has been involved in an affair must be removed. (That goes for the senior pastor, ministers, trustees, and officers as well.)

The Scripture goes on to state that you must handle your financial affairs properly. Any deacon who is not a tither needs to be removed. Deacons who have experienced a foreclosure or filed for bankruptcy or has a poor credit score needs to be removed.

The Scripture says that you must manage your children properly. If any deacon has children who have been suspended, dropped out from school, illiterate, or incarcerated, he should be removed.

Let's go further. If you interpret 1 Timothy 3:1–13 literally, then this Scripture would have excluded Paul, who was not married, David, who was involved in an affair with Bathsheba, and Peter, who had a terrible temper.

That said, I am willing to compromise if you must exclude deacons from the list. But I wanted to at least challenge you on even this last bastion of power. The ultimate goal is for teens to be involved in as much of the running of the worship service as possible. I'm completely confident, and the research supports this, that if they feel like valued members of the church community we will increase the likelihood of them staying in the church.

The teen empowerment model goes much further than just having them involved in the worship service. Teens should be involved in all operations of the church. I want all their gifts and talents to be stirred up. Listed below are the church operations they can help support.

- Internet, including the church's Web site, Facebook page, and Twitter account
- Office staff
- Maintenance
- Visitor follow-up
- Creation of a bulletin, including graphic design and writing
- Leadership board
- Hospitality committee
- Missions
- Retail
- Day care
- Kitchen

Chapter 8: Teen Empowerment Model

Teens should be a part of every ministry in the church.

The New Role of the Youth Pastor and Youth Ministry

There is a tendency among senior pastors and churches to resist youth participation in the main sanctuary. Interestingly, youth pastors and the youth ministry industry at large resist as well. Youth ministry is a multi-billion dollar industry. There are thousands of youth pastors, numerous conferences, workshops, magazines, journals, and books. They too are interested in the preservation of the status quo. In this book I've commended youth pastors for the great work they are doing, but I'm also challenging them. If we continue to take the position that this is the way we've always done it while hoping and praying for a different outcome, this borders on insanity.

My model assigns a new role to youth pastors. If teens are in the main sanctuary during the worship service that means youth pastors are no longer giving a sermon to teens on Sundays. However, that does not end your work with teens. They must be prepared to serve with adults, and they must be transitioned into the larger church. You will still give the sermon to junior high school students.

First, to ensure that the new mission, goals, and objectives are on track, I would encourage youth pastors to adapt the following list to evaluate the effectiveness of their ministry. I want you to develop this progress report for each youth.

WHAT IS THE ROLE OF TEENS IN YOUR CHURCH?

Six-Year Progress Report—7th to 12th Grade

Parents
- Parents' names and contact information _____
  _____
- Parents' faith, maturation, and biblical background
  _____

Teens
- Name: _____
- Salvation: _____
- Baptism: _____
- Bible literacy: _____
- Devotional time: _____
- Love for Jesus: _____
- Prays with authority: _____
- Understands righteousness: _____
- Understands and receives power from Holy Spirit
- Walks by faith: _____
- Understands the power of words and confession: ____
- Believes in absolute Truth: _____
- Speaks in his/her heavenly language of tongues: _____
- Strengths: _____
- Weaknesses: _____
- Church ministries: _____
- Church mentor: _____
- Healthy friendships: _____
- Peer pressure: _____
- Leadership: _____
- Selflessness: _____
- Grades: _____
- Career goals: _____
- Time management: _____
- Has become a disciple: _____

Chapter 8: Teen Empowerment Model

Prior to high school graduation, conduct exit exams with your seniors. Asking questions such as the following will give you invaluable information on the effectiveness of your youth ministry.

1. How do you respond to someone who says they will go to heaven because they are a good person and they help people?

2. Do you believe all religions serve the same God?

3. Why do you have to go to church?

4. Why are so many Christians hypocrites?

5. How do you, as a Christian, feel about premarital sex, homosexuality, alcohol, smoking, and hard drugs?

6. How are you going to handle college or the workforce with so many unbelievers? What would have been your response to the professor and the president of Northwestern University after the classroom intercourse demonstration?

The following are the new tasks of the youth pastor.

Teen Assimilation Coordinator. I commend my church in Phoenix, Arizona, Faith Christian Center, for having a Volunteer Assimilation Coordinator. Every person who becomes a member of the church takes a talent survey so that the Volunteer Assimilation Coordinator can ascertain the new members' strengths and weaknesses, their desires, gifts, and talents. The Volunteer Assimilation Coordinator sits down with the new member, along with a survey and a list of church ministries in hand, and they discuss where his or her strengths and gifts can best be utilized. This is an excellent design, and I recommend that youth pastors do the same. Schedule time to sit down and talk to teens about where they would like to serve in the adult church. Set up a mechanism where teens and the various church ministries are connected. Let them know they can always come to you if they need to talk.

Coordinate mentorship program. A report from the Carnegie Council on Adolescent Development found that significant adult-youth relationships forged in religious youth work had a more positive impact on youth development than any other youth ministry delivery system.[42]

The youth pastor should identify adults to serve as mentors to teens, and each teen should be assigned an adult mentor. The youth pastor would coordinate and follow-up on the progress of mentor-mentee relationships.

Lead and conduct forums on hot teen topics, including sexuality, dating, bullying, academics—whatever concerns youth, parents, and the larger church. Even though the teens are now members of the larger church, you will still have access to the youth during these various forums. They could be held during the week, either on a Wednesday or Saturday morning or afternoon.

Recreation and social events. This includes movies, bowling, roller skating, and ice skating, etc., but I want to do something different here. So many times in the recreation ministry the youth have their activities, and the adults have theirs. The adults have their bowling league, and the teens

Chapter 8: Teen Empowerment Model

have theirs. The adults have their baseball or volleyball team, and the teens have theirs. I want to be consistent in this teen empowerment model. I see no reason why the adults have their basketball league, and the teens have theirs. Let teens and adults enjoy sports together, and there are many ways we can do this. Have two basketball teams of five players each, with teens and adults on each team. Or the adults can play the teens. The main thing is that we're having fun together. Only seven percent of teens' waking hours outside of school are spent with adults. The church has been a victim in this age segregation as well. Recreation ministry is an excellent, fun way to increase the time teens spend with adults.

There will be times when youth pastors will want to do teen-specific events. For example, I love lock-ins and holy hip hop events, and teens enjoy them, too. In holy hip hop events, teens are invited to come to the church on Saturday night, and from 8:00 to 12:00 p.m., they have praise and worship, play video games, listen to music, roller skate, eat pizza—whatever they enjoy. Then the females go off into one area with their sleeping bags, and the males go off into their area. At 7:00 a.m. they are awakened, have breakfast, and then they are walked into the sanctuary for the 8:00 a.m. service. By giving young people something to do on a very critical, often dangerous night of the week, holy hip hop and lock-ins reduce crime and a lot of problems in our communities. It's an excellent idea that needs to be planned and coordinated by the youth pastor.

Missions/Camps/Retreats. They are great ways to remove youth from the familiar and into a more immersive, intensive worship experience.

> "Religious camps have impressive records of helping teens become more intentional about devotion, more secure in their faith identities, and therefore more confident and explicit in telling the God-story of their tradition. Those churches with the largest numbers of highly devoted teens were the most likely to send their teens to camp."[43]

In his excellent book *Uncommon Youth Ministry,* Jim Burns shares the following story:

> "Some years ago Cathy and I took a trip with eight high school students. We traveled 1500 miles for Bible study and to do a service project. It was a three week drama of loving, service, tension, rowdiness and sainthood all wrapped up in one experience. Today all eight of those students are in some form of Christian ministry. I believe they chose to be in ministry as adults because they had a chance to have their hearts broken with what breaks the heart of God when they were in the impressionable years of adolescence. Getting young people involved in missions and service is a key necessity for Christian growth and maturity."[44]

Chapter 8: Teen Empowerment Model

The youth pastor will also be involved in missions. I've read a lot of literature that suggests that almost more than any activity, missions work really engages teens and keeps them in church. When young people get away from the familiar (negative peer group) and go off into the mission field with other believers for a period of time, this is a powerful experience. Many youth have said it had a major impact on their lives, and they were never the same. I strongly suggest that we take our youth away from the familiar as often as possible.

Does your church do missions work? Are your teens involved?

Let me describe two examples of great missions work that are being led by young people: See You at the Pole and the Agape Community Kitchen.

"See You at the Pole was started in 1990 by some teens in Burleson, Texas. One Saturday night they felt compelled to pray, and so they went to three different schools and prayed at each school's flagpole. From there a challenge was issued to students throughout Texas to meet at their flagpoles and pray simultaneously. So at 7 a.m. on September 12, 1999 over 45,000 students met at their flagpoles to pray before school.

"The concept ballooned from there. Word spread quickly across the U.S., and youth ministers reported that students outside of Texas had heard about the event and were feeling the same burden for their schools as these Texas students had.

"On September 11, 1991 the students got their national day of prayer, as over one million students from all around the country gathered around their flagpoles at 7 a.m. to pray. Today that number has grown to 3 million students in the U.S. and there are also students in 20 other countries that participate in the event."[45]

Another group of teenagers felt moved to start the Agape Community Kitchen.

"Every Wednesday night teen volunteers at the Agape Community Kitchen in Westfield, New Jersey, prepare and serve a nutritious meal to 250 people in the nearby town of Elizabeth. Teenagers started and continue to lead this soup kitchen ministry, which also provides a clothing closet for guests to receive blankets, clothes, and shoes. What began as a Presbyterian youth group's hands-on service activity has become a weekly way of life priority where for almost a decade has attracted a very diverse corps of teenage volunteers. Young people were drawn to an activity that matters, that makes a difference in the world."[46]

When young people are no longer spectators and actually serving others, whether in evangelism or missions work, they do a tremendous job.

"The organization Passion recently hosted a global gathering in Atlanta of over 23,000 college students who consider themselves Christians. Instead of the typical Christian conference with the consumers' appetite for great speakers and music, they made the centerpiece of these four days the 'Do Something Now' campaign. They put eight global opportunities on the table and said to students, we think you have the money in your pockets to change the world. And sure enough, they responded. Those poor college students pledged or gave over $1 million to build 52 wells in Africa, to provide New Testament translations for six people groups of Indonesia, and to combat the human sex trafficking industry."[47]

It's exciting to get young people involved in ministry. When teens are involved, there are no limits. They have the energy and desire to do missions. They don't understand what the word "no" means. They sincerely believe that "I can do all things through Christ who strengthens me" (Philippians 4:13). I'm just excited about all the opportunities we have in our churches to get young people off the bench and into the game and do all the things that they can do.

Deliver the sermon. The youth pastor should be expected to deliver the sermon in the main sanctuary from time to time.

Integrate youth into larger church's music ministry. Music is such an important part of the worship service that I wanted to highlight it. Music that teens enjoy should be considered, and teens should be involved in all choirs, orchestras, and bands. I'm advocating for a full integration of young people into all the choirs of the church, and the youth pastor should coordinate this integration with the Music Director. Whether your church has one choir or many, teens should be included so that they can praise the Lord in song. Some of the larger churches have a children's choir, a teen choir, an adult choir, a senior choir (co-ed), a men's choir, and a women's choir. Except for the children's choir, all choirs should be integrated. Your men's choir should include teens so that 16-year-old teen males are singing with 65-year-old males. Sixteen-year-old teen females are singing with 65-year-old female elders in the women's choir. The main choir should not just be reserved for adults 21 and over. If your teens have excellent voices, they need to be a part of the main choir.

That means the teen choir will be completely folded into one of the other adult choirs. In other words, there will be no more teen choir. If you are concerned about self-preservation and holding on to certain aspects of ministry, I encourage you to let go and let God.

One of the major reasons some adults do not want to worship with young people is that they don't like their music, and this goes both ways. Teens are bored with the hymns, and the elders have a disdain for gospel rap. We need to listen to each other. If young people are one-third of the world's population, then at least one-third of the music in the church should be geared toward young people. There are gospel rappers out there who are clean, unashamed to call His name Jesus, washed by the Blood, and their music needs to be a part of the worship service. Listed below are some of the teen Christian musicians and groups that should be considered. Because teen culture is always changing, this list is only being provided as a sample. In a year or two the list will be obsolete, but please understand the principle behind the list, which is that teen music must be included in the main worship service.

DISCLAIMER: I cannot endorse every song by every artist because I do not know if every song they have ever done is clean. However, many of the popular, clean tunes by the following artists are loved by Christian youth and have a powerful, positive impact on their walk with the Lord.

- Amy Grant
- Avalon
- Big Daddy Weave
- Britt Nicole
- By The Tree
- Casting Crowns
- Charlie Hall
- David Crowder Band
- Disciple
- Flyleaf
- Hillsong
- Jeremy Camp
- LA Symphony
- Lecrae
- Matt Redman

- New Breed
- Skillet
- Starfield
- Stellar Kart
- Steve Fee
- T-Bone
- TobyMac
- Tripoli
- Unhindered
- Gospel holy hip hop CDs

Coordinate theological growth and development. There is a theological crisis in youth ministry. How can we expect teens to participate passionately in praise and worship when some do not know Who they are praising? Some teens have told me no one ever asked them in youth church if they wanted to be saved. This is amazing and very disappointing. I recommend the following strategies to address this problem.

Awana. I'd like to commend Awana Clubs International. Based in Chicago, Awana is an organization with fully integrated evangelism and discipleship programs for children and youth ages two to 18 that actively involve parents, church leaders, and mentors. Awana services more than 17,000 churches.

"In 2007 an independent research firm conducted a nationwide survey of adults ages 19 to 32 who participated as kids in an Awana ministry for six to 10 years. The 720 respondents had all earned awards in Awana for their active participation in Awana curriculum, knowledge of scripture, and consistent attendance. 92.7 percent said they still attend church week services."[48]

Study of Exemplary Congregations. Developed from the survey results of the 131 exemplary congregations and on-site interviews with 21 of these congregations, this study identifies 44 aspects of faith that contribute to the spiritual growth and development of young people.[49]

The study identified seven characteristics that youth pastors and churches should consider in their planning. I encourage you to read this study in full detail. The seven characteristics are as follows:

1. Seeking spiritual growth
2. Possessing a vital faith
3. Practicing faith in the community
4. Making faith a way of life
5. Living a life of service
6. Exercising moral responsibility
7. Possessing a positive spirit.

In *The 7 Checkpoints of Spiritual Development* by Andy Stanley, the characteristics are:

1. Authentic faith – Do your teens trust God?

2. Spiritual discipline – Are they having devotion on a regular basis?

3. Moral boundaries – Are they setting boundaries and limits?

4. Healthy friendships – Are they selective with their friends?

5. Wise choices – Do they consider the future with present decisions?

6. Ultimate authority – Do they believe in absolute truth?

7. Others first – Do they practice selflessness, not selfishness?[50]

Coordinate youth training in the main church's Foundation Ministry. The purpose of any church's foundation ministry is to teach new members "what we believe"; it lays a solid foundation for success in the lives of the believer and creates a biblical hunger and desire for God's will. Teens should be thoroughly trained in your church's statement of belief.

To be a member of my other church, Living Word Christian Center in Forest Park, Illinois (Bill Winston is the pastor), you must take the following 11 Foundation Ministry classes that are on tape. Review the classes and see how you might adapt them to your youth training program.

Salvation One & Two – Total redemption has been provided to all who believe and accept Jesus Christ because of His life, death, and resurrection. This teaching explains the total plan of redemption and all its benefits.

Chapter 8: Teen Empowerment Model

Holy Spirit – This teaching offers a clear explanation of the importance of Holy Spirit and the difference between the "with-in" and the "upon" experience for every believer.

Prayer – It is not surprising that many of us are not aware that there are different types of prayers with various applications for those prayers. In this teaching, promises in the Word of God are given, as well as the basis for the different types of prayers and their various applications.

Faith – The Bible says, "The just shall live by... faith" (Habakkuk 2:4). This teaching explains what faith is, how a person obtains faith, how to use faith as a servant, and much more.

Covenant – The highest agreement that one can make on earth is a covenant. This teaching fully explains God's covenant, the reason for the covenant, and how you can have a covenant relationship with God.

Healing – Healing is a provision of salvation! Learn what the Word of God has to say about healing and divine health.

Prosperity – For too long the Church has been viewed as not having enough. This teaching will erase all wrong thinking about prosperity and wealth and truly teach you how God wants you to prosper according to His Word.

Righteousness – This is the foundation for walking in "great" faith. This tape sets the tone for knowing our Kingdom rights, the benefits we partake of by being joint-heirs with Jesus. This teaching also teaches what righteousness is and what righteousness is not.

WHAT IS THE ROLE OF TEENS IN YOUR CHURCH?

Evangelism – The great commission! God expects all born-again believers to be effective witnesses. This teaching concludes the Foundation Training Series with an upbeat and stirring message "Go ye into all the world and preach the Gospel to every creature."

These classes are designed to produce mature disciples. I define a babe in Christ as someone who only received the gift of salvation. The mature saint prays with authority, has a lifestyle pleasing to God, understands the power of confession, and knows God wants them healed, financially prosperous, and walking in love. Mature saints walk by faith and stand on the Word. The world gives our youth education. We must expose them to Holy Spirit who will give them *revelation*. We must help teens understand they have two natures. Paul describes them in Romans 7 and 8. One nature is ruled by the flesh and the other by the Spirit. The one who is fed the most will dominate. I am confident we will see churches with teens on fire for God who will surpass many elders who are ruled by their flesh.

It is only the church that is keeping teenagers back as spectators. In every other field—business, science, the military, journalism, medicine, education, entertainment, and sports—teens are encouraged to reach their full potential. It is only the church that holds teens back. This practice must come to an end.

Some of the most successful people did outstanding things while they were still teenagers (there are even some children on the list). If you don't believe me, read the following inductees in my **"Teens Hall of Fame."**

- **DR. KEITH BLACK**, neurosurgeon – began surgery at age 15 on dog
- **GEORGE WASHINGTON**, first president – surveyor at age 17
- **CLARA BARTON**, founder of the Red Cross – began nursing at age 11
- **ALEX AND BRETT HARRIS**, bestselling authors – founded The Rebelution at age 17
- **THE LATE JOSHUA GUTHRIE** – provided 900 million gallons of clean water overseas at age 18
- **ZAC SUNDERLAND** – sailed the world solo at age 17
- **TIGER WOODS**, golfer – turned pro at age 19
- **VENUS WILLIAMS**, tennis star – had professional debut at age 14
- **SERENA WILLIAMS**, tennis star – debuted professionally at age 14
- **MICHAEL JACKSON**, music star – started at age 9
- **BIBLICAL JOSHUA** – assistant to Moses as a teenager
- **BIBLICAL DAVID** – killed Goliath between ages 10 and 17
- **KOBE BRYANT**, NBA star – entered the NBA at age 17

- **LEBRON JAMES**, NBA star – entered the NBA at age 18

- **OPRAH WINFREY**, billionaire/media mogul – career began at age 19

- **SMOKEY ROBINSON**, singer – started career at age 16

- **THEODORE ROOSEVELT**, president – became a body builder at age 12

- **MARTIN LUTHER KING**, civil rights leader – gave his first sermon at age 17

- **PAUL MCCARTNEY**, singer – started his career at age 15

- **JOHN QUINCY ADAMS**, president – part of diplomatic mission to Russia at age 14

- **LAURA WILDER**, famous writer – taught school at age 15

- **DAVID FARRAGUT**, first U.S. Navy Admiral – cadet at age 12

- **LOUIS LATIMER,** scientist – lieutenant in the Navy at age 16

- **NELSON MANDELA**, president – participated in anti-apartheid school boycott at age 19

- **PHILLIS WHEATLEY**, writer – began writing poems at age 13

- **JUSTIN BIEBER**, singer – started singing at age 12

- **WOLFGANG MOZART**, composer – composed his first symphony at age 8

- **BILL GATES**, inventor – started Microsoft at age 19

- **TREVOR FERRELL**, advocate – founded Trevor's Place to feed the homeless at age 12

- **JOHN WESLEY**, cleric and theologian – launched the beginning of the Methodist movement at age 17

- **ALBERT EINSTEIN**, scientist – wrote his first scientific paper at age 16

- **STEVEN SPIELBERG**, filmmaker – directed his first film at age 16

- **MARK ZUCKERBERG**, online inventor – launched Facebook at age 19

- **LOUIS BRAILLE**, inventor – designed a system of reading for the blind at age 15

- **JOSIAH, KING** – became king of Israel at age 8; began reforming the country at age 16

- **JOAN OF ARC**, warrior – led 3,000 French knights into battle at age 17

- **MOTHER THERESA OF CALCUTTA**, nun – started her work in India at age 19

- **ELVIS PRESLEY**, singer – started his career at age 19

- **JADEN AND WILLOW SMITH** began acting at ages 5 and 7, respectively

- **SELENA GOMEZ** began acting at age 7

Now identify 20 more famous people who started their careers during their teen years.

I'd like to close this chapter with the following youth confession. Your teens should confess this statement daily.

YOUTH CONFESSION

The Bible tells me don't let anyone look down on me because I'm young. I am a warrior of God. I am a joint heir with Jesus. God has a wonderful plan for my life. I am God's workmanship, created for good works. He told me to stir up my gifts, and they will make room for me. I am fearfully and wonderfully made. I will delight myself in the Lord, and He will give me the desires of my heart. I have been bought with the Blood of Jesus. I will not smoke, drink alcohol, or consume illegal drugs. I will abstain from sex until marriage. I can do all things through Christ who strengthens me. Amen!

We will now move to the most important chapter of the book, New Wine, New Wineskins.

Chapter 9: New Wine, New Wineskins

What good is it to hear a sermon if you do not practice the sermon? What good is it to read a book, but you don't implement the ideas from the book?

Throughout this book you've been presented with a problem: 40 percent of middle school students leave the church by eighth grade, and 70 percent of female teens and 90 percent of male teens leave by high school graduation. We have reviewed numerous reasons for their exodus: age segregation, tradition, power, ego, and the theological crisis in youth ministry. In the last chapter, we offered an empowerment model that not only will empower teens in the worship service but in every operation of the church.

John 8:32 says, "And you shall know the truth, and the truth shall make you free." What does this mean? Smokers know there's a good chance they will die of cancer. One-third of all smokers die of the disease. It is only when they stop smoking that they reduce their risk of getting lung cancer. Applying the truth to their lives makes them free.

We know that fruits and vegetables are good for us but junk food is not. Exercise is good for us; being sedentary is not. It's not enough to *know* that exercise and eating fruits and vegetables are good for us. It's actually exercising and eating fruits and vegetables that give us good health. This is the truth making us free.

WHAT IS THE ROLE OF TEENS IN YOUR CHURCH?

As I have mentioned throughout this book, apprenticeships and internships with adults are far better for our teens than peer pressure. Will the church begin to implement such programs? That would be the truth setting churches and youth ministries free.

As Jesus says in Luke 5:37–38, "No one puts new wine into old wineskins; or else the new wine will burst the wineskins and be spilled, and the wineskins will be ruined. But new wine must be put into new wineskins, and both are preserved."

The youth empowerment model is what I'm calling "new wine," and it cannot be poured into old wineskins—that is, the old wineskin of "This is the way we have always done it." The old wineskin of "I want to implement this model, but my denomination would not approve it." The old wineskin of "The elders don't want to worship with youth." The old wineskin of "If we bring the teens into the sanctuary there will be less space available for visitors." The old wineskin of "If we bring the youth in, there may be an exodus of elders, and elders give more money." The old wineskin of loss of funds. The old wineskin of age segregation. The old wineskin of "We don't want to expand our music comfort zone." The old wineskin of "Youth ministry has its own autonomy; that should be good enough." The old wineskin of "I'd have to make the sermon palatable not only for the 65-year-old female but the 16-year-old male. That would place a greater burden on me."

I understand I'm asking a lot of senior pastors, but you are the shepherds of your churches. After all is said and done,

God is going to hold you accountable for your flock. He didn't say your flock of elders. You are the pastor for the entire church. God is going to hold you accountable for the 40-70-90 Teen Exodus.

But I believe something new and wonderful is occurring even as I write these words. "God is not *the author* of confusion but of peace" (1 Corinthians 14:33, NKJV). He is giving one message and one message alone to the church about the spiritual development of our teens. Teens *are* very important, so there must be more attention, funding, resources, square footage, and teaching devoted to our teens. We must develop rites-of-passage celebrations that transition teens into the adult congregation. We must help our teens mature spiritually under the guidance of adult mentors.

I am excited about what is going to take place in your church. Can you imagine how many young Davids, Esthers, Peters, and Marys are in your church? Can you just imagine the great work that is going to be done by your youth in the worship service, missions, and all aspects of church service? I'm excited about your church becoming a beacon of hope in your neighborhood. Even better than in the business, medicine, sports, and entertainment arenas, young people will reach their full potential and all their gifts will be stirred under the guidance of Holy Spirit. Praise God!

I recently heard a powerful sermon titled "Go Hard" from Minister Erica Moore at my Phoenix, Arizona church Faith Christian Center. She shared the following story.

"A student on fire for Jesus filled with Holy Spirit with the evidence of speaking in tongues was in tears of joy in class. The teacher asked the student to leave and go to the restroom to get herself together. After several minutes when she had not returned, the teacher sent another student to see if she was okay. When they did not come back, the teacher continued sending students. When almost the entire class had not come back, the teacher went to see and found the entire class was having praise and worship and giving their lives to Jesus!"

When our youth have a personal relationship with Jesus, even when they are in a place where He is not welcomed, prayer is not allowed, and the Bible has been removed, our youth can be the Light.

I want to commend the youth of Egypt for spearheading the revolution there. They were able to overthrow a 30-year dictatorship. It also shows the power of the Internet, Facebook, Twitter, and YouTube when used for a righteous cause. And if youth can overturn governments, surely they can play a more active role in our churches.

I believe we can reverse the 40/70/90 percent exodus. I really believe that we can flip the script, and instead of 40/70/90 percent leaving, those same numbers are now staying. Can you imagine the kind of power, the kind of ministry you can have if your teens are staying?

Chapter 9: New Wine, New Wineskins

And finally, I'd like to say to teens, my prayer is that you never let anyone cause you to disdain or look down on your youth. Look to Jesus as your guide and your model. Jesus went into the temple at the age of 12, and that's when you need to enter the temple. My prayer is that you never leave Jesus, you never leave His church, and you never become lukewarm. May you always be passionate about your Lord and Savior. Go hard after God. I can assure you that He is passionate about you! May you live a life full of joy, peace, and power. God bless you!

Afterword

I have mentioned throughout this book the great work churches are doing for teens. Thousands of youth are on the mission field and at retreats and camps. I have also mentioned the great work teens are doing. I commend the organizers of See You at the Pole. I included Alex and Brett Harris in our Teen Hall of Fame for their great work and the founding of Rebulution. I just want to add a few more. I encourage all of you to view the video Empty produced by Ryan Shook a teenager and the son of pastor Kerry Shook. Ryan explains that youth are empty and are looking in all the wrong places for fulfillment. Congratulations to Vy Higginsen who founded in 2006 Gospel for Teens. They are doing a great job of bringing teens all over New York to sing for Jesus. Last, I want to commend the organizers of the Alive Festival . This Christian music concert tour is attracting over 3 million youth annually. I commend all teens who are doing great things to share the gospel of Jesus Christ.

Endnotes

1. Ham, Ken. *Already Gone.* Green Forest: Master Books, 2009, pp. 25, 31.
   King, Mike. *Presence Centered Youth Ministry.* Downers Grove: IVP Books, 2006, p. 24.
   Dyck, Drew. *Generation Ex-Christian.* Chicago: Moody, 2010, p. 17.
   The data shows 80% of teens leave and most youth ministries are two-thirds female. Therefore the inference is 70 percent females and 90 percent males leave the church.

2. Dean, Kenda. *Starting Right.* Grand Rapids: Zondervan, 2001, p. 197.

3. ibid. p. 215
   Ham, Ken. op. cit. p. 10.

4. Fast Facts about American Religion.
   www.hirr.hartsem.edu/research/fastfacts.

5. DeVries, Mark. *Family Based Youth Ministry.* Downers Grove: InterVarsity, 2004, p. 102.

6. New Study Shows Trends in Tithing.
   www.barna.org/barna-update. USA Today March 14, 2011. p. 9a

7. Ham, Ken. op. cit. p. 57.

8. King, Mike. op. cit. p. 46.
   Dean, Kenda. *Almost Christian.* New York: Oxford, 2010, p. 6.

9. Schultz, Thom and Joani. *Kids Taking Charge.* Loveland: Group Books, 1991, p. 24.

10. Dean, Kenda. *OMG.* Nashville: Abingdon, 2010, p. 21.

11. Lawrence, Rick. *Jesus-Centered Youth Ministry.* Loveland: Group Books, 2007, pp. 35-36.

Endnotes

12. McDowell, Josh. *Right from Wrong*. Plano: W. Publishers, 1994, p. 308.

13. Kinnaman, David. *Unchristian*. Grand Rapids: Baker Books, 2007, p. 122.

14. Kimball, Dan. *They Like Jesus But Not the Church*. Grand Rapids: Zondervan, 2007, p. 36.

15. Lyons, Gabe. *The Next Christians*. New York: Doubleday, 2010, p. 40.

16. McDowell, Josh. op. cit. p. 68.

17. ibid. pp. 12, 246.

18. Calhoun, Mike. *Pushing the Limits*. Nashville: Nelson Books, 2006, p. 22.

19. Considering Homeschooling Ministry. www.christianhomeeducation.org/publicschools.

20. *U.S. Statistical Abstract 2010: The National Data Book*. Washington: Census Bureau, 2010.

21. Ham, Ken. op. cit. pp. 88-89.

22. Dean, Kenda. *OMG*. op. cit. p. 14.

23. ibid. p. 14.

24. Kinnaman, David. op. cit. p. 47.

25. Reid, Alvin. *Raising the Bar*. Grand Rapids: Kregel, 2004, p. 97.

26. DeVries, Mark. op. cit. p. 73.

27. Fast Facts about American Religion www.hirr.hartsem.edu/research/fastfacts.

28. Dean, Kenda. *OMG*. op. cit.

29. Johnston, Kurt. *Best Practices for Youth Ministry*. Loveland: Simply Youth Ministry, 2010, p. 95.

30. Fields, Doug. *Purpose Driven Youth Ministry*. Grand Rapids: Zondervan, 1998, p. 87.

31. Ham, Ken. op. cit. p. 29.

32. Fields, Doug. op. cit. p. 46.

33. Schultz, Thom and Joani. op. cit. pp. 103-104.

34. Lawrence, Rick. op. cit. p. 146.

35. U.S. Statistical Abstract 2010.

36. Elmore, Tim. *Generation iY*. Atlanta: Growing Leaders, 2010, p. 63.

37. ibid. p. 63.

38. Kunjufu, Jawanza. *Reducing the Black Male Dropout Rate*. Chicago: African American Images, 2010, p. 116.

39. The Importance of Fathers. www.laughyourway.com/blog/the-importance-of-fathers.

40. Recording Industry Association of America. www.riaa.com.

41. Dean, Kenda. *The Godbearing Life*. Nashville: Upper Room Books, 1998, p. 85.

42. The Mosaic of Faith-Based Mentoring. www.educationnorthwest.org.

43. Dean, Kenda. *Almost Christian*. op. cit. pp. 154-155.

44. Burns, Jim. *Uncommon Youth Ministry*. Ventura: Regal, 2001, p. 140.

45. See You at the Pole.
www.christianteens.about.com.

46. Dean, Kenda. *OMG*. op. cit. p. 31.

47. Kinnaman, David. op. cit. p. 143.

48. Awana Alumni Study.
www.awana.com.

49. Effective Christian Education.
www.searchinstitutepress.org/faith.

50. Stanley, Andy. *The Seven Checkpoints for Youth Leaders*.
New York: Howard Books, 2001, pp. 10-12.

Bibliography

Burns, Jim. *Uncommon Youth Ministry: Your Onramp to Launching an Extraordinary Youth Ministry*. Ventura, California: Regal/Gospel Light. 2001.

Calhoun, Mike. *Pushing the Limits: Unleashing the Potential of Student Ministry*. Nashville, Tennessee: Nelson Books. 2006.

Dean, Kenda. *Almost Christian: What the Faith of Our Teenagers is Telling the American Church*. New York, New York: Oxford University Press. 2010.

Dean, Kenda. *OMG: A Youth Ministry Handbook*. Nashville, Tennessee: Abingdon Press. 2010.

Dean, Kenda. *Practicing Passion: Youth and the Quest for a Passionate Church*. Grand Rapids, Michigan: Wm. B. Eerdmans Publishing Company. 2004.

Dean, Kenda. *Starting Right*. Grand Rapids, Michigan: Zondervan/Youth Specialties. 2001.

Dean, Kenda. *The Godbearing Life: The Art of Soul Tending for Youth Ministry*. Nashville, Tennessee: Upper Room Books. 1998.

DeVries, Mark. *Family-Based Youth Ministry*. Downers Grove, Illinois: InterVarsity Press. 2004.

DeVries, Mark. *Sustainable Youth Ministry: Why Most Youth Ministry Doesn't Last and What Your Church Can Do About It*. Downers Grove, Illinois: IVP Books. 2008.

Dunn, Richard R. *Shaping the Spiritual Life of Students: A Guide for Youth Workers, Pastors, Teachers & Campus Ministers*. Downers Grove, Illinois: InterVarsity Press. 2001.

Dyck, Drew. *Generation Ex-Christian: Why Young Adults Are Leaving the Faith—And How to Bring Them Back*. Chicago, Illinois: Moody Publishers. 2010.

Elmore, Tim. *Generation iY: Our Last Chance to Save Their Future*. Atlanta, Georgia: Poet Gardener Publishing. GrowingLeaders.com. 2010.

Bibliography

Fields, Doug. *Purpose-Driven Youth Ministry: 9 Essential Foundations for Healthy Growth*. Grand Rapids, Michigan: Zondervan/Youth Specialties. 1998.

Fields, Doug. *Your First Two Years in Youth Ministry: A Personal and Practical Guide to Starting Right*. El Cajon, California: Zondervan/Youth Specialties. 2002.

Ham, Ken. *Already Gone: Why Your Kids Will Quit Church and What You Can Do to Stop It*. Green Forest, Arkansas: New Leaf Publishing Group/Master Books. 2009.

Ham, Ken. *Raising Godly Children in an Ungodly World.* Green Forest, Arkansas: New Leaf Publishing Group/ Master Books. 2008.

Harris, Alex and Brett. *Do Hard Things: A Teenage Rebellion Against Low Expectations*. Colorado Springs, Colorado: The WaterBrook Multnomah Publishing Group. 2008.

Johnson, Kurt. *The 9: Best Practices for Youth Ministry*. Loveland, Colorado: Simply Youth Ministry. 2007.

Kimball, Dan. *They Like Jesus But Not the Church: Insights from Emerging Generations*. Grand Rapids, Michigan: Zondervan. 2007.

King, Mike. *Presence-Centered Youth Ministry: Guiding Students into Spiritual Formation*. Downers Grove, Illinois: IVP Books. 2006.

Kinnaman, David. *Unchristian: What a New Generation Really Thinks about Christianity—And Why It Matters*. Grand Rapids, Michigan: Baker Books. 2007.

Lawrence, Rick. *Jesus-Centered Youth Ministry*. Loveland, Colorado: Group Publishing. 2007.

Loewen, Wendell. *Beyond Me: Grounding Youth Ministry in God's Story*. Scottdale, Pennsylvania: Faith & Life Resources. 2008.

Lyons, Gabe. *The Next Christians: The Good News about the End of Christian America*. New York, New York: Doubleday Religion. 2010.

McDowell, Josh. *Right From Wrong: What You Need to Know to Help Youth Make Right Choices*. Nashville, Tennessee: Word Publishing Group. 1994.

Myers, William R. *Black and White Styles of Youth Ministry: Two Congregations in America*. Eugene, Oregon: Wipf and Stock Publishers. 2005.

Oestreicher, Mark. *Youth Ministry 3.0: A Manifesto of Where We've Been, Where We Are & Where We Need to Go*. Grand Rapids, Michigan: Zondervan/Youth Specialties. 2008.

Olson, Ginny. *Youth Ministry Management Tools*. Grand Rapids, Michigan: Zondervan/Youth Specialties. 2001.

Reid, Alvin. *Raising the Bar: Ministry to Youth in the New Millennium*. Grand Rapids, Michigan: Kregel Publications. 2004.

Rice, Wayne. *Reinventing Youth Ministry (Again): From Bells and Whistles to Flesh and Blood*. Downers Grove, Illinois: IVP Books. 2010.

Riebock, Josh. *My Generation: A Real Journey of Change and Hope*. Grand Rapids, Michigan: Baker Books. 2009.

Robbins, Duffy. *This Way to Youth Ministry: An Introduction to the Adventure*. Grand Rapids, Michigan: Zondervan/Youth Specialties. 2004.

Robbins, Duffy. *Youth Ministry Nuts and Bolts, Revised and Updated: Organizing, Leading, and Managing Your Youth Ministry*. Grand Rapids, Michigan: Zondervan/Youth Specialties. 2010.

Schultz, Thom and Joani. *Kids Taking Charge: Youth-Led Youth Ministry*. Loveland, Colorado: Group Publishing. 1991.

Senter, Mark. *Four Views of Youth Ministry and the Church*. Grand Rapids, Michigan: Zondervan/Youth Specialties. 2001.

Senter, Mark. *When God Shows Up: A History of Protestant Youth Ministry in America (Youth, Family, and Culture)*. Grand Rapids, Michigan: Baker Academic. 2010.

Stanley, Andy. *The Seven Checkpoints for Youth Leaders: Seven Principles Every Teenager Needs to Know*. West Monroe, Louisiana: Howard Books. 2001.

Notes

Notes